36.95

Praise for

Action Reflection Learning

"The application of the ARL process ensures that the important issues get addressed, that people are committed to outcomes, and that business results are achieved."

—Angela Hyde, vice president, Global Learning & Development, AstraZeneca

"This book unfolds the dynamics and principles of Action Reflection Learning very much the way it all came to me and my team at Motorola when I was working with high-potential managers. I continue to use and recommend ARL."

—Bob Aron, PhD, director, New Product Development, DeVry University

"Rimanoczy and Turner's ARL approach to learning is innovative, revolutionary, and applicable to this generation of knowledge workers. Finally, a book that articulates a fresh methodology along with the rigor and quintessence necessary to make a significant impact."

—Lisa Brooks Greaux, director, Executive Development, Pfizer, Inc.

"ARL operates in the heart of the action, as a team does its actual work. It's not just reflective planning before a project begins (which is what commonly passes for 'action learning' in corporate leadership programs), nor is it just reflection on lessons learned after the project is done."

—Grace Nakar, Wells Fargo Technology Talent Management and Executive Development

"The authors communicate their extensive experience with ARL programs in a way that infuses the book with their spirit as well."

—Lyle Yorks, associate professor, adult learning and leadership, Teachers College, Columbia University

"Rimanoczy and Turner have done a masterful job in capturing the essential theories and principles that make ARL so valuable."

—Michael Marquardt, president, World Institute for Action Learning

"Finally, a book on ARL! In this very readable book that emulates the ARL approach, Rimanoczy and Turner demonstrate how practitioners can learn experientially through an organized adult educational process."

—Joe Raelin, Asa Knowles Chair of Practice-Oriented Education, Northeastern University; author, *Work-Based Learning* and *Creating Leaderful Organizations*

"Rimanoczy and Turner use adult learning theory to frame their innovative approach to training and development, creating a much-needed paradigm shift in the field. *Action Reflection Learning* encourages facilitators to create meaningful programs that address real problems."

—Patricia Cranton, visiting professor of adult education, Penn State University at Harrisburg; author, *Understanding and Promoting Transformative Learning*

"An extremely readable and creative presentation of practical strategies for enhancing adult learning. It offers fresh and accessible insights into ARL and how to apply it in a range of interpersonal settings."

—Jeanne E. Bitterman, lecturer, Department of Organization and Leadership, Teachers College, Columbia University

"Offers a blended approach to learning that accommodates different learning styles."

—Ted Nguyen, editor, *The O.D. Journal;* former chair, Global Committee on the Future of OD

"By advocating the use of real day-to-day problems and opportunities for learning in the workplace, together with details of well-proven methodologies, it shows how organizations can minimize waste in learning transfer."

—Bryan Smith, independent consultant; editor, Industrial & Commercial Training; author, *Developing Managers Through Project-Based Learning* and *Project Based Learning for Developing Managers*

Action
Reflection
Learning™

Action

Reflection

Learning™

**SOLVING REAL BUSINESS PROBLEMS
BY CONNECTING LEARNING WITH EARNING**

ISABEL RIMANOCZY & ERNIE TURNER

Davies-Black Publishing
Mountain View, California

Published by Davies-Black Publishing, a division of CPP, Inc., 1055 Joaquin Road, 2nd Floor, Mountain View, CA 94043; 800-624-1765.

Special discounts on bulk quantities of Davies-Black books are available to corporations, professional associations, and other organizations. For details, contact the Director of Marketing and Sales at Davies-Black Publishing: 650-691-9123; fax 650-623-9271.

Visit the Davies-Black Publishing Web site at www.daviesblack.com.

Printed in the United States of America.
12 11 10 09 08   10 9 8 7 6 5 4 3 2 1

Library of Congress Cataloging-in-Publication Data
    Rimanoczy, Isabel.
    Action reflection learning : solving real business problems by connecting learning with earning / Isabel Rimanoczy and Ernie Turner. — 1st ed.
      p. cm.
    Includes bibliographical references and index.
    ISBN 978-0-89106-240-0 (hardcover)
    1. Adult education. 2. Business and education. 3. Employer-supported education. I. Turner, Ernie. II. Title.
    LC5225.E57R56 2008
    374—dc22
                                              2007031298

FIRST EDITION
First printing 2008

Contents

Figures and Tables

Tables cont'd

Preface

"Do three things: Write a book, plant a tree, have a child." Popular sayings carry wisdom, and this one, claimed to be of both Talmudic and Chinese origin, invites us to transfer knowledge, sustain the earth, and sustain the species. Following that wisdom, in this book we seek to transfer our combined experience and knowledge about learning to a new audience.

What exactly is Action Reflection Learning™ (ARL™)? What are the characteristics? Does it have a common definition? How is it done? What are the key success components? Why does it work? What is the foundation of this practice?

ARL is a holistic learning methodology based on reflecting, alone and with others, on real actions, on personal experience. For many years, ARL practitioners have been generating know-how in different locations and in different settings. Lessons have been accumulated, sometimes shared, sometimes forgotten. Several practitioners have reflected about their experiences and tried to organize and describe them in handbooks, papers, and articles. A few have researched aspects of the ARL practice in order to further the understanding.

Before the conceptual framework for it was developed, ARL seemed impossible to grasp, to define—as singular as an experience, different in each case, changing each time. Research revealed that some practitioners described it as an art, a magic result of the individual experience, talents, gifts, knowledge, and personality. Others elected to respond by narrating what they did, hoping the actions would be self-explanatory. Some handed out a copy of a workshop design or an agenda, or listed some tools that they introduced. Some preferred to describe the reactions of the learners, others' epiphanies, and still others' feedback. Some avoided explanations altogether.

The research brought some answers, which in turn generated the conceptual framework, which led to the theoretical foundation of the ARL practice. Isabel Rimanoczy and Boris Drizin developed a conceptual architecture that could explain the practice. Then, along with Paul Roberts, they further refined it. The explanations were not the ultimate answers, but they were an attempt to describe and organize what practitioners have been doing. And we realized that this practice was actually a learning methodology.

After we presented our findings to different ARL practitioners to validate our reflections, we were encouraged to write about the methodology. While a book on ARL had been a pending project for several years, this seemed to us to be the right timing. We had some theory to share with our growing practice.

This book is an invitation to join us on a learning journey. We thought that the best way to share ARL was to follow the ARL sequence as much as possible.

One of ARL's characteristics is the attention paid to learning style preferences so that diversity is honored when learning interventions are designed. Therefore, we structured this book to accommodate those who are interested in the "why" questions (purpose, rationale, and deeper meaning), those who are more curious about the "what" questions (facts, theories, and data), those who are more intrigued by "how" questions (processes, designs, tools, and techniques), and those who are more captivated by the "so what" questions (practical applications and variations). We offer stories, rationales, theories, tools, and hints for application. We also selected a diverse way of communicating these stories; you will find traditional case narratives, dialogues, and even a journal entry approach.

Part 1 of the book sets the stage. We begin with a brief vignette to take you straight into someone's life. Then we reflect on it and extract lessons, introducing some considerations about adult learning and the origins of ARL.

Part 2 is all about action and stories. The ARL elements are shared in a just-in-time fashion, as they emerge in the narrative.

The journey will take you to different locations and a variety of settings where ARL has been applied. We assume that as you progress in this journey, you will become more and more familiar with the ARL components. Thus we move progressively from describing them in context to merely calling them out.

Part 3 lets you hear the voice of the Learning Coach, the ARL practitioner. We share stories that portray the Learning Coach in action and simply indicate where an ARL element is being used.

Part 4 is for those who want to know the conceptual framework, the theoretical underpinnings of ARL, and want to dive deeper into the origin of this learning methodology. We explain in depth the assumptions behind the elements and in what phases they are most often applied: discovery, planning, design and redesign, learning interventions, and evaluation and debrief. We share the theoretical foundation that sustains the ARL practice and describe in detail the roles of the Learning Coach, indicating the knowledge, skills, and mind-sets appropriate for that function.

Enough said. As more than one practitioner has noted, to understand ARL, you need to experience it.

Acknowledgments

Writing this book has involved many people. I, Isabel, would like to thank Clara Arrocain, who felt that I had to write a book many years before I had even dreamt of it. Also, I want to thank Krystyna Weinstein, who challenged an early version of our book project when we didn't have sufficient research to support it. A similar seed was planted by Guadalupe Martinez de Léon, who wondered what was behind Action Reflection Learning, and Rafael Echeverría, who asked similar questions as he tried to understand what this practice is all about. I have to thank them for inspiring me to undertake the research—the cornerstone around which this book was built. I also thank Jeffrey Keefer, who, with his curiosity and questions, pushed me to put all those thoughts into writing, as he kept wondering, Where can I read about this? Why is this not published? I thank Boris Drizin, who partnered with me in the virtual journey of creating the conceptual framework of ARL, and Paul Roberts, whose further explorations into the theoretical foundations are reflected in chapters 11 and 12. I thank my friend and professor Lyle Yorks, who read my first articles about the conceptual framework and gave me encouragement and guidance. And I thank Lennart Rohlin, who supported this project and ensured that the story of the MiL Institute was well told.

I also want to thank my family and friends for their personal support, and especially my partner in both work and life, Ernie Turner. He introduced me to a new world, in many senses, and ARL was a part of it.

I, Ernie, want to thank my original LIM partners—Lars Cederholm, Tony Pearson, and Victoria Marsick—who pioneered ARL in the United States and joined me along with our MiL colleagues in putting the *R* in ARL. Without the inspiration and energy of this original team, we would not have arrived where we are today. Lennart

Rohlin, in particular, has served as a mentor and role model throughout our twenty-one years of doing this exciting work. As an experiential learner, I've learned most of what I know of this practice from my clients and colleagues. There are too many of you to mention individually, but special gratitude goes to the following: Jackie Turner, who helped me discover so much about the relationship between teaching and learning in the jungles of Borneo, Angola, Kenya, and Brazil; Lynn Gray, who invited me to join him in one of my greatest learning opportunities ever, working inside the public schools, where I discovered so much about the work I'm doing today; Eva Arnell, for the many years we worked and learned together; Angela Hyde, Urban Skog, Robin White, Rod Stull, and Andrew Webster, among others, who invited me to partner with them in many exciting learning challenges; and Chris Dennis and Pedro Mata, who went out on a limb and allowed us to work with LIM in making their merger work. And last, but most important, to Isabel, who took the lead on this project and provided the inspiration, coaching, and leadership. Without her patience and persistence, this book would not have been written. Thank you!

And we both want to express our special gratitude to the editing team of Paul Roberts, Boris Drizin, and Tony Pearson, who added invaluable input and comments; and to Jeffrey Keefer, Judy O'Neil, Lyle Yorks, Jeanne Bitterman, and Victoria Marsick for their suggestions. This book would not be what it is without the careful professional editing of Chris Murray and Mark Chambers and the encouragement of Chuck Palus, Martin Wilcox, and Connie Kallback, who saw the diamond in the rough. Laura Lawson provided enthusiastic support from the very beginning, and Laura Simonds contributed with savvy guidance. To our partners, Willie Anderson, Tony Pearson, and Ronald Waugh, we owe gratitude for their continued encouragement and support. To our teachers, the hundreds of participants in all the interventions we have designed and delivered, and the colleagues with whom we've teamed, we express our deep gratitude.

About the Authors

Isabel Rimanoczy is a Legacy Coach and a partner at LIM (Leadership in International Management), a global network of coaches who provide a variety of interventions and strategies focused on developing leaders, teams, and organizations using Action Reflection Learning (ARL) principles. She is also the director of IFAL—USA (International Foundation for Action Learning). She has worked in organizational analysis and diagnosis, change and transition management, recruitment, coaching, and executive development for multinational corporations in North America, Latin America, Europe, and Asia. She has trained more than two hundred Learning Coaches and presented at numerous conferences around the world.

Rimanoczy received a BA degree in psychology from the University of Buenos Aires and an MBA degree from the University of Palermo, and she is currently a doctoral candidate in the Adult Learning and Leadership Program, Teachers College, Columbia University. She is coauthor of the *LIM Learning Coach Handbook* and *Leader Coach Handbook,* author of the *Handbook for Mergers and Acquisitions,* and editor of the electronic newsletter "LIMNews." In 2005 she received an author scholarship from the Sven Ake Nilsson Memorial Fund in Sweden for her contribution to knowledge development and scientific innovation.

Ernie Turner has served as president of LIM for more than twenty years. He has written numerous articles on teamwork and leadership and was a contributor to the book *Earning While Learning in Global Leadership.* Over the past thirty years he has worked with more than one hundred teams in thirty different countries from a wide variety of organizations and at all levels.

Previously Turner worked for eight years as a teacher and school principal in the United States, Malaysia, Angola, Brazil, Italy, and Kenya, followed by ten years as an educational consultant for the New York City school system, where he was one of the creators of an innovative approach to school reform. During this time he gained valuable experience and insights into the relationship between teaching and learning that are employed today in ARL principles and practices.

Turner received a BA degree in English literature from Wheaton College and an MA degree in educational administration from City College, New York. He is a frequent speaker and presenter on leadership, teamwork, and engaging the workforce.

PART ONE

Adult Learning and Action Reflection Learning (ARL)

We begin this section with a full immersion into an everyday scene, a vignette in which learning and its challenges are presented as they happen in real life. We will come back to this vignette later, analyzing and making more meaning out of it. Bear with us.

Next, we share with you different perspectives and reflections about adult learning. What is it, how does it take place, and what are the best and the most efficient ways for learning to happen? What works and what does not? You will find a brief introduction into the origins of ARL, its evolution, and the main differences between it and traditional training. Not too much, just enough to get you ready to see how ARL is used in action.

A Learning Story

Let's look at Jack, a businessman in a real-life learning situation.

A bird's warbling had roused Jack from sleep. For some time, the bird had been part of a dream, but then somehow it became more insistent, and he woke up. "What bird is that?" he wondered, in a mixture of anger and curiosity. "And why is it singing at night!?" Slowly, he half-opened an eye and noticed it was light outside. He grumpily turned to his night table to glance at the alarm clock.

Oh, no! It was 7:30! Jack jumped out of bed. Why hadn't the alarm rung? His sister Rose had given him this new clock for his birthday, and last night he decided to replace his old one with this elegant new one. "Too many buttons," he had thought, as he struggled to set it. What had happened to the old, simple alarm clocks? Life is getting more and more challenging. Cell phones have more features than he can handle. In the past few years, the techno-geist had multiplied: computer programs, the digital camera, the DVD player, the new iPod, the LCD projector, even the wireless laptop require technical expertise. And now alarm clocks! Is this progress? He wondered when his golf clubs would become programmed and electronic. Wouldn't that be nice? They could jump out of the bag by sensing the distance to the green and the terrain. "That reminds me," he thought, "I have to stop at the pro shop. I heard from Jimmy about this new driver they're offering. He says his game has improved so much—and, in fact, I've seen it! That's worth a little investment," he mused, justifying the expenditure to himself.

"No time for coffee," he thought, dressing hastily. As he walked out, he picked up the newspaper and glanced at the headlines. No time for news either—he'd get his update from the radio while driving. As a VP of marketing in a real estate business, he had to stay on top of the news. Trends in the economy, regulations for investors, immigration changes, oil prices, international crises, environmental campaigns, consumer prices—everything had an impact on his business. He recalled the problems he'd had a few years ago when he indulged himself with two weeks in Polynesia. He had seen so many advertisements for this earthly paradise, and after doing some research on the Internet, he gave himself the gift of a vacation of "total disconnect." Hadn't that been a wonderful experience! Except that because he hadn't read the news for more than fourteen days, he'd missed the announcement of a major competitor opening its offices in town. His whole marketing campaign for the quarter would have been a total loss if he had not hurriedly changed it.

Actually, there had been some minor damage: He'd had a tough conversation with his boss, who blamed him for being irresponsible. That discussion lingered for a long time in his mind. He had hated it, because it resonated with the blame his father always laid on him. Is that karma? Maybe there was some truth in it, a pattern. But were those "real" vacations a sign of irresponsibility? After all, he had noticed the problem before it was too late. Alicia had mentioned the news in a casual water-cooler conversation. Talk about just-in-time!

Alicia. That reminded him to confirm with her his participation in the negotiation workshop. Alicia was in charge of training, and she had invited him to a two-day course on negotiation. He had been evasive for some weeks, as he really wasn't very interested. Negotiation? What was so special that he had to invest two full days in it? He normally didn't have problems getting what he wanted, one way or another. He liked to study the problem and be creative in finding attractive solutions—and he was proud of his friendly attitude, which was, in his opinion, the key to good negotiations. "That's something I got from Mom!" he realized with a smile. Unlike his sister Rose, who was constantly in conflict with everyone around her. "We are so different," he mused. If only she could take the course for him!

Alicia was a good colleague. She was always forwarding him information about events in the city, many of which he really enjoyed. "That's not part of her job, after all. She's in training, and the events she keeps mentioning are about networking gatherings or other community-related meetings." He felt obligated to attend this negotiation course, in return for all the attention Alicia had paid him. "This is when I would need negotiation skills," he said to himself with a laugh. "So I don't have to waste two full days sitting in that course! Well, let's just do it, and who knows, maybe I can get something out of it anyway."

CHAPTER 1

A Different Approach to Adult Learning

Adults mostly learn automatically through the experiences, realities, and needs of their daily lives. Action Reflection Learning (ARL) builds on this automatic learning and captures it through the reflective process, converting that tacit knowledge into conscious learning (see Figure 1). As we will see in the following chapters, ARL fits the pragmatic requirements of the business world, which demands learning that can be quickly applied and retained for later use.

FIGURE 1. **The Action Reflection Learning (ARL) Cycle**

According to Benjamin Bloom, learning can be categorized in three psychological domains:[1]

- **Cognitive Domain:** related to the acquisition and application of knowledge and understanding. For example, reading about the various forms of karate is cognitive learning.

- **Affective Domain:** concerned with attitudes and feelings resulting from the learning process. For example, through karate classes students develop an attitude of persistence and patience.

- **Psychomotor Domain:** concerned with physical skills. Mastering the kicking, punching, and blocking skills taught by a karate instructor is an example of psychomotor learning.

ARL integrates Bloom's three domains into one methodology of learning.

Let's return to our story of Jack, the adult learner. Glance at the story now and estimate the number of learning situations in which Jack has found himself. Now check your estimate against the actual number: seventeen. Surprised? You identified the negotiation course—that's the traditional schooling method of learning. However, in this story, Jack is learning almost constantly in many other ways. He reports learning how to manipulate electronic devices. He experimented with the devices in his attempts to figure them out, using a trial-and-error method. He learns about golf—by listening to the advice of his friend and the pro shop and by imitating what he sees in the hope of improving his drive.

Jack also learns important information that affects his business, by reading newspapers and listening to the radio. He learns about vacation options from ads in the media and by active exploration on the Internet. He learns about how he is being perceived through conversations with his boss and his dad, and he increases his self-awareness through reflection and critical thinking. He extracts lessons from experience by looking back and reviewing events, establishing cause–effect connections that guide him in future situations, trying to avoid what didn't work well. "Is it OK

to disconnect during vacations?" he wonders. He learns peripher-
ally by being with others and adopting behaviors, like the friendli-
ness of his mom. He detects areas of ignorance by asking himself
questions about birds; he learns about differences among individuals by reflecting on the puzzling behaviors of others, like his sister Rose. All this learning, without taking a course. Jack is learning
continuously, most of the time without realizing he is learning.

Jack's morning demonstrates the action foundation for ARL,
where ARL reaches in to capture the learning that is happening.

THE TEACHER/CLASSROOM APPROACH

When most people think of learning, they think of something
very different from what Jack experienced. What comes to mind is
schooling in a formal classroom setting in which professors or experts teach an audience of students. Teachers present what they
know in a more or less attractive way so that students can learn.
Learning is frequently seen as a result of study—in other words, a
result of paying focused attention to a specific topic in order to
memorize it. This cognitive process of acquiring information in-
cludes listening, taking notes, asking questions, and reading. The
information is stored, ready to be retrieved whenever we need to
apply it.

The institutionalized schooling system, as Peter Vail notes, has
been built on the assumption that there is good, valid objective
knowledge and that expert individuals can share this knowledge
and pass it on to the audience, who will in turn receive it, assimi-
late it, and use it at their convenience.[2]

In this paradigm, experts identify what needs to be "known,"
then learning professionals define learning *goals,* the *contents* of
the courses or training sessions that will lead to those goals, and
the best *methods* for conveying those contents. Let's say, for example, that experts identify the ability to coach as a key leadership
skill. A learning goal could be that a person masters the art of

coaching. The contents could be about communication, feedback, dynamics of change, or different types of questions. Methods could include lectures, role play, video recording, exercises, and so forth. When colleges and universities prepare syllabi for students or training professionals prepare programs for organizational audiences, they are establishing the goals, contents, and methods for the courses. Those professionals also decide how to evaluate the learning.

LEARNING OUTSIDE THE CLASSROOM

The teacher/classroom approach is not intrinsically bad. However, it is not the only approach to learning, and, depending on the individual or the circumstances, it may not be the best. Classroom learning tends to focus on the Cognitive Domain of learning without using the Affective or Psychomotor Domains.

Research on learning indicates that individuals have different learning styles and preferences.[3] Those who prefer to learn facts and data are best suited for the traditional classroom setting. Those with pragmatic preferences, who want to know how they can use what is taught or why it is important, may have a more difficult time. Those who need to experience, to try out, to involve not only the mind but the feelings, the senses, the emotions, or the intuition also don't fit easily into the traditional classroom learning approach.

Some experts who are exploring the learning experience from the learner's perspective see classroom-style learning as ineffective, especially for business situations. They see students memorizing and repeating information, only to forget much of it shortly after the test. Graduation is an administrative step for an external purpose, such as getting the necessary credential for a job. Little attention may be given to how the information connects to the lives and realities of the students. This disconnect is what Jack, the protagonist in the story, anticipates from the negotiation course and why he is not enthusiastic about it.

John Dewey, one of the most influential educators and philosophers in American history, explored the process of adult learning and highlighted the importance of experience in guiding our present actions.[4] Dewey believed that we make meaning by creating explanations of events and that we use those explanations as behavioral guides. The explanations are actually our personal interpretations: We build explanations using our own impressions, lessons learned, advice received from others, and even our imagination and creativity.

Most of that processing happens in an automatic way, of which we are only partially aware. We don't think of this as learning. Even if Jack were to read his own story, he would find at most one or two snapshots that he would relate to learning. He sees Alicia's recommendations of networking meetings in town as a nice gesture, not related to her training position. Reading newspapers and thinking about his mom or about birds are probably not recognized as learning events either.

And yet . . . These many daily automatic processes help us tackle the challenges of life—to deal with objects, with others, with ourselves. We absorb information permanently, and without much conscious processing it becomes knowledge. We construct cause–effect relationships with the hope that they will help us obtain what we need. When we are faced with something unexpected, we look for explanations. When we are faced with something strange or new, we look for known data, for similarities to something familiar.

MAKING OUR AUTOMATIC LEARNING MORE EFFICIENT

Visualize your mind as an immense warehouse, where new entries are stored every second. Multiply that by days and then by years. Plus, those entries self-organize and begin to interact with other entries, grouping themselves in multiple creative ways. When we are facing a dilemma, we automatically reach into that warehouse to find information that helps us address the situation. But the warehouse, containing millions of entries, is also understaffed. As a consequence, we don't get all that we have stored or necessarily get the most suitable resource. Like Jack, when faced with tough feedback from the boss we may retrieve a father's blaming comments—which may make us feel worse about the boss. We may even react to the boss as we would to our dad.

When we can consciously identify learning experiences that occur during the day, we are able to "label" the entries as we find them a short distance into the warehouse and organize them better. Now think of the learning activities in which you have participated and consider how many times you have been able to make this conscious entry, labeling what you are storing. When we hear a speaker, we process the words as we connect what is being said with our own reality: with our experience, questions, or challenges, with our interests or our emotions. These "connected" entries are the ones that are most useful.

In many adult learning situations, little time is reserved for these essential connecting and labeling components of the learning process. Why is so little attention given to the audience members' need to make meaning of what they are experiencing? We are left alone to take care of that task. In a two-hour presentation, the mind's warehouse has received multiple entries, say, one every few seconds. That makes 1,400 entries. No wonder we don't "learn" from this learning: Who has the time to go back and bring order to that?

Jack showed us seventeen learning-related snapshots—without being aware of it. He learned from *experience,* from *others,* from *reading,* from *reflecting,* from *asking questions,* from *trying out,* from *thinking creatively,* from *imitating,* from *listening,* from *exploring,* from *talking,* and from *receiving advice.* He learned with his mind, his body, and his emotions. All of this was timely and relevant. These are certainly more exciting ways to spend a day than attending a negotiation workshop. No wonder he doesn't want to attend.

What would adult education be like if all these different ways of learning were included in programs designed for adults? This is the story of ARL.

CONNECTING LEARNING TO OUR REALITIES

Development of ARL began in the late 1970s through the efforts of a group of professors at the University of Lund, Sweden, friends in management positions, and colleagues who were consultants and HR professionals. They were brought together by common frustrations with the behavior of managers and with the ways in which training programs were addressing the professional development of executives. This avant-garde group came up with a different way of training, one that focuses on learning rather than on teaching.

It is no surprise that ARL emerged from the business arena. Organizational training involves a client–vendor relationship. In consumer-oriented Western society, this relationship created a setting in which the buyers (and later the training participants) were progressively seen as customers whose needs determined the added value of the program. In the beginning, the approach was most similar to Action Learning.[5] Over time, the training activities began to be more sensitive and adjusted to the needs, interests, and reality of the buyer and the participants. For example, practitioners have adapted the length of the programs to the busy agendas of participants, trying to cover more in a shorter time. Increasingly, corporate clients ask for facilitators with experience in their own industrial areas, ensuring that the training will be customized with the language and examples of the industry. And solving actual business problems is a key characteristic of ARL programs.

Over the years, ARL has evolved into a learning methodology, applied in a diversity of settings. It has been used for a number of purposes that have one thing in common: Something has to be learned. For example, it has been used for the following purposes:

- To help individuals learn to work together in postmerger integration
- To help teams learn how to handle conflicts or crises
- To prepare young talent for the next challenges
- To help learn how to implement performance appraisal processes
- To develop synergy in regional teams
- To design conferences, courses, and meetings

SUMMING UP

The differences between classroom-style learning and ARL are profound, as outlined in Table 1. But rather than describing ARL's differences, let's see them in action.

TABLE 1. **Some Differences Between Traditional Training and Action Reflection Learning (ARL)**

TRADITIONAL TRAINING	ACTION REFLECTION LEARNING
Generalized objectives	Co-designed, learner's ownership
Segmented	Integrated
One size fits all	Conscious of learning and personality styles
Focus on skills or knowledge	Focus on skills, knowledge, mind-sets, attitude, and behavior change
Teaching by experts	Learning with coaches
Just-in-case training	Just-in-time learning
Case studies, hypothetical situations	Current challenges
Knowledge oriented	Knowledge, learning, and action oriented

PART TWO

The Learning in Action

In this section, you will find stories and vignettes that portray the learning in action. As part of the journey we promised, you will have the opportunity to glance into different types of learning settings. You will see Learning Coaches working with executives to help in a postmerger integration; visit an Asian leadership team preparing for a transition; observe an MBA course being taught using ARL in a Latin American country; witness the learning process at a very problematic high school in New York; watch how leadership skills are developed in a group of school superintendents; attend a professional conference session in Colombia organized as a learning intervention; and even observe a motivational session for a sales force in a Middle Eastern country. These are all true stories, with the names modified for privacy purposes.

A Brief Note About the Pedagogic Sequence

Rather than follow the traditional pedagogic sequence of providing information, giving examples, and asking you to apply what has been taught, we have chosen to follow the ARL sequence. We take you to the stage of the action, periodically stop to reflect briefly on what is happening in the story, and elaborate further on the theory at the end. The chapters in parts 2 and 3 also follow a sequenced progression; in the early chapters, we highlight most of the sixteen ARL elements as they occur in each story. After that we simply call them out, as you will have become familiar with them.

CHAPTER 2

A Successful
Merger

In the early 1990s, George, the chairman and CEO of a U.S. multinational corporation, decided to go into the coffee business. This idea came to him after he had enjoyed a particularly delicious coffee dessert. Thus inspired, George sent Raul, a trusted president who was leading one of the businesses, with the company checkbook to buy enough commercial companies to give George global market share.

Raul set off into what was a new world for him and soon acquired three companies in the commercial business—one in the United States, one in Latin America, and one in Germany. As each of these companies had also recently expanded by acquiring another company, the three companies really represented six companies—each with its own culture, customers, and plants scattered across sixteen different locations on five continents—plus their own products, some competing and some complementary. Adding to the complexity, the presidents of these three companies were of very different nationalities—one was British, one was German, and one was Spanish.

George was pleased when he learned that these acquisitions gave his company a respectable market share in a completely new industry and in a gesture of acknowledgment invited Raul, of Hispanic origin, to become the CEO of this new organization—

Global Coffee. Raul accepted the challenge of merging the six companies into one integrated company.

Raul assembled his new team—the three existing presidents plus a VP for finance and a VP for human resources and organizational development (OD) from the United States. From the start, the executive team seemed to do well in its periodic meetings. However, two years later, the desired cultural and business process integration across the six companies had still not taken place, and the anticipated business synergies were not being realized. Although the executive team made sound business decisions, its members' direct reports and those on the level below them were slow to implement the decisions. There was a general lack of cooperation and no real "buy-in" to the merger. It seemed that executive team members had not been able to convince their direct reports of the rationale for following through.

Concerned by the situation, Adam, the VP for HR/OD, decided to conduct a culture survey. The results confirmed what he had suspected. A number of areas needed attention if the company were to prosper: teamwork was poor; trust had to be developed; communications were ineffective; conflicts were not well managed; innovation in strategic thinking and action was lacking; and change management skills and processes had yet to be developed. If Global Coffee were to become a truly global company with the flexibility and ability to leverage all its assets (people, plants, products, processes, and customers) quickly, it needed more than the executive team's lip service; the entire organization needed to think and act differently. Major change was required, and the team's direct reports were the key.

TURNING TO ACTION REFLECTION LEARNING FOR HELP

It was at about this time, two years after the deal was done, that a consultant who had been working with the executive team suggested that Raul and Adam use ARL to help with the integration.

He thought that an approach to organizational development that combined development of leadership skills and work on actual organizational challenges might provide part of the solution to Global Coffee's global integration challenge.[6] Raul contacted us, and together we formed an ARL team with Adam from Global Coffee and three lead consultants.

The team worked on the core business question "How can we engage the direct reports of the executive team and their direct reports in developing and then executing the needed changes?" These second and third levels of the organization formed a group of approximately sixty individuals who were very influential in the organization. The ARL team designed a leadership development program, the New Leadership Program (NLP), that used existing business and organizational challenges as the arena for learning.

A PROGRAM FOR ALL NEEDS

The objectives of the NLP addressed multiple needs:

- Socialize this influential group so that members get to know and trust one another

- Solve current organizational and business challenges that are sitting in the executive team's lap and have prevented the merger from really working

- Develop team skills and leadership skills (influence, consulting, problem solving, project management, decision making, conflict resolution, change management, etc.) while working on these challenges

- Learn how to manage across matrix, functional, cultural, and geographic borders

- Understand and appreciate the complexity of the commercial coffee business by working shoulder to shoulder with individuals from different parts of the business

Ownership of the Learning

Results of Adam's culture survey plus the recommendations for training needs showed that the desire for change and the need for change were both there. The combined "push-pull" provided the perfect foundation for an emerging strategy designed by the ARL team.

Balancing Task and Learning

Building the learning process on actual business and organizational challenges made the process more compelling and memorable for the learners.

- Recommend changes that will make Global Coffee more competitive and profitable

Based on the desired outcomes, the ARL team designed the NLP for these managers, reasoning that they would be the de facto implementers of the organizational change strategy and that they therefore needed new leadership competencies, skills, mind-sets, and behaviors in order to lead the change process.

GETTING BUY-IN FROM
THE EXECUTIVE TEAM

Adam and Raul were quickly convinced of the merits of this change strategy on paper, particularly since they helped co-design the NLP. However, Raul still had to convince his executive team that this was a good investment of time and money, and he was not clear on a Learning Coach's roles and scope of interventions. To address this concern, and because it was critical that the executive team be familiar with the dimensions and language of ARL, the ARL team proposed that we spend a weekend working with the executive team during one of its quarterly off-site meetings so that team members could experience the type of support a project team might get.

This proved to be an effective solution, offering an experiential understanding of the function of the Learning Coach. The meeting provided multiple learning opportunities, and it took only half a day for the team to appreciate the value the coaches had brought.

The off-site meeting was scheduled to begin at 8:30 A.M. on Friday. The first ones to show up for the meeting were the German president and his VP. The two of them were already there when we arrived around 8:15. Everyone else except Raul arrived by 8:25, and after fifteen minutes of standing around and chatting over cups of coffee, people began to take their seats. We could sense a

Just-in-Time Intervention

Incidental learning opportunities require just-in-time readiness. Some of the best lessons arise out of the work and natural flow of the session. We were ready to anticipate and catch those moments as they occurred.

real uneasiness in the room, especially with the two German executives, who kept looking at their watches, indicating their impatience. Around 8:45, Raul arrived with a big smile on his face and a warm welcome but no excuse or rationale for being late. The German executives were not happy.

After getting a cup of coffee and a brief review of the agenda, Raul turned to us to remind the team of our role as Learning Coaches. We briefly explained that we were there as observers who would occasionally interrupt the meeting when we thought there could be an opportunity for learning or introducing a concept or tool that might make the meeting more efficient.

By then there was some real concern about the number of items on the agenda and the lack of time. It was 9:15, and they were just beginning the meeting.

Just before the morning coffee break, we approached the table and asked if the participants could take ten minutes for a quick debrief of how they felt the team was performing. We then asked them to take a minute to identify one thing they felt was going well so far in their meeting and one thing they felt could use improvement. After a minute's reflection, they went around the table and exchanged ideas about the things that were going well.

We participated as well. Then team members exchanged ideas on what could be improved. It just so happened that the German president began, and he spoke passionately about a pattern they had adopted as a team of beginning the meetings late and how frustrated this made him. The others all nodded, and most of them mentioned punctuality as a key area for improvement. Raul seemed a bit surprised and asked us, after everyone had spoken up, "And now what do we do with this?"

Realizing that there were some major cross-cultural gaps within the team in relation to time, we asked if team members had agreed upon team norms. A few said "No," while others asked, "What are norms?" We explained that when a team takes time to make explicit the norms or behaviors expected of its members, then it is easier to hold one another accountable. And usually, team norms

> **Appreciative Approach**
>
> **Guided Reflection**
>
> Through the guided reflection question, we helped the team identify those teamwork processes that seemed to be working. Sometimes people are not aware of the little things they do that make a positive difference. An appreciative approach to feedback is motivating not only to the individual who made the difference but to the other team members as well. When good behavior is acknowledged, it is frequently adopted by others.

Safe Environment

Freedom to speak up is vital for high performance. The fear of retribution or censoring, real or not, often inhibits individuals from saying what is in their hearts and on their minds. As Learning Coaches, we initially provided the opportunity and "space" for members of the team to feel free to speak up and register whatever feelings of discomfort or unease they might have. Then we helped team members define the conditions that would allow them to create their own safe environment for speaking up when we were no longer with them.

Unfamiliar Environments

Familiarity breeds complacency. Unfamiliar environments in which individuals work on projects outside their experience alongside those from different regions and functions can generate creative thinking and rich incidental learning.

promote higher team performance. We then offered to help them set up their own norms after the break if they thought this would be helpful. Everyone agreed that it would be. The break provided a perfect time for everyone to think about a behavior or two that would help all of them work more effectively as a team. And after the break, it took only fifteen minutes to get everyone's input and agree upon a set of desired team behaviors. Of course, punctuality was among them.

The second half of the morning meeting had a much more open and respectful feel to it. The tension was gone; there was greater focus on the business issues. And the team was consciously attempting to act according to its newly agreed-upon norms, which had been posted in a visible location.

During the course of the next two days, we also helped the team streamline both its decision-making process—we had noticed that they had difficulties reaching agreement—and its meeting management process, after observing that some practical tips could be welcome. As we noticed that the extraverts were dominating the discussions, we offered a very effective technique for ensuring equal participation around the table. By the end of the meeting, every member of the team had a real appreciation for the added value Learning Coaches could bring to a team, and they all voiced their full support for proceeding with the NLP.

READY TO MOVE ON

After this positive experience, the executive team provided its full support for the NLP program.

The ARL team divided the group of sixty participants into three subgroups of twenty participants, ensuring that each subgroup had representatives from each of the acquired entities and that there was as much diversity as possible—in function, national culture, geography, gender, and so on.

Importantly, Raul explicitly instructed the teams that he was as interested in what each team and individual learned as much as in the proposed solutions to the challenges. For him, there was a 50/50 balance between learning and project solution. This was an enormously powerful message for participants, who, based on their work history, had been rewarded for taking action, and for achieving results.

The design that flowed from this learning objective had the following elements:

- There were four five-day sessions spread over a seven-month period.

- Each session would be held in a different location where Global Coffee did business.

- Each group of twenty was subdivided into four teams of five. The teams were asked to self-select based on the following criteria: the choices must (1) maximize the team's diversity and (2) exclude any team member with functional expertise in the business challenge assigned to the team. This arrangement encourages innovative thinking, cross-functional learning, leading through influence, and cross-organizational consulting. If an individual had experience in the project undertaken, there would be a danger that other team members would defer to him or her; new ways of addressing problems would be lost; and team members would not develop the critical thinking faculties that are essential for any change process.

- Each team was given a project—a current business challenge with global or regional scope and complexity to solve.

- Each business challenge had a "client"; the executive team members initially served as clients for the first NLP.

- Each team had a Learning Coach whose job was to help the team stop, reflect, and exchange feedback and insights on a

Sequenced Learning

Repetition reinforces learning. The ARL team was interested in applied learning, so it ensured through the program design that participants had opportunities to try out what they learned from one module to the next. This kind of repetition supports an individual in going from awareness to conscious application to unconscious mastery.

Learning Coach

Reflection usually takes discipline. As team members naturally get drawn into the task, Learning Coaches were "contracted" to encourage them to focus periodically on how they did what they did and what they were learning about themselves, leadership, teamwork, and so on. The Learning Coaches would also help them identify opportunities for applying what they had learned.

Ownership of the Learning

It would be the responsibility of each participant to identify his or her learning goals based on the numerous inputs and then ask for help—from the team, the coach, and colleagues.

periodic and as-needed basis on a variety of processes—teamwork, leadership, consulting, organizational effectiveness, personal learning goals, and professional competencies.

- Teams were given approximately half of the twenty formal program days to decide how they would spend that time working on their business challenges; they spent an equal amount of time or more between the sessions on various activities related to their projects.

- The other half of the program was used for large group sessions that addressed preplanned topics that had been identified in the needs assessment and organic topics that arose during the life of the program. The ARL team used members of the executive team and others inside the company as subject matter experts as much as possible in order to give them the exposure they needed and to maintain the proper Global Coffee focus and context.

- Each individual worked on a personalized learning plan that was influenced by a 360-degree assessment in addition to team feedback, supervisor input, learning partner input, and personal coaching from the Learning Coach.

ATTACKING THE MAJOR BUSINESS CHALLENGES

Most of the projects for the first NLP focused on the unachieved expectations or synergies that had been envisioned as reasons for the merger.

One project dealt with fulfilling the unmet needs of customers and suppliers. The team members were an HR compensation and benefits manager from the U.S. headquarters organization, a VP of finance from the U.S. business, a business development director of U.S. origin from the German business, a French director of operations, and a German plant manager. No one was from Customer

Satisfaction. Their client, the German VP, told the team, "It is absolutely vital that we find out what our customers and suppliers really want and then use this information to fortify our competitive position. We must use a systematic approach to get them on our side, form working partnerships, and be preferred above all other service providers. Being the best in satisfying needs serves to 'build a brick wall' around our customers and suppliers, keeping them in the GC fold and driving the competition out." The team's challenge question was "How can we meet the unsatisfied needs of our customers and suppliers?"

Team members interviewed internal customers, external customers, vendors, and other members of the NLP. They visited nineteen major customers located in four countries. In order to establish best practices outside the industry, they interviewed and visited four non-coffee companies with excellent reputations for fulfilling customer needs. Most of the footwork was done between the four formal sessions so that when the entire team was together, it could focus on analyzing, preparing recommendations, and extracting lessons at multiple levels with the Learning Coach.

At the final session in the fourth week, the team made its recommendations to its client and the executive team along with the other three teams. The recommendations addressed both the hard issues (quality, service, reliability, and technical services) as well as the soft issues (open communications, trust, building rapport, and ethics). The team specifically recommended forming cross-divisional teams composed of individuals responsible for dealing with customer and supplier needs on a daily basis. And the executive team designated a representative group from the NLP who also worked in this area daily. Group members were responsible for supporting the cross-divisional customer/supplier team to ensure that all the recommendations were addressed.

Another team was responsible for streamlining the procurement process. During their project work, team members discovered with surprise that all six entities that formed the merged company were purchasing coffee beans from the same suppliers using different standards, processes, pricing, and contacts. Likewise, no one from Procurement was a member of this team. Within the first week, the team had identified a savings opportunity worth $380,000, more than the cost of the NLP.

Other teams worked on the following projects:

- Defining quality for the company

- Identifying logistical cost savings

- Reducing costs in finance and administration

- Creating an organization that identifies and realizes global synergies on a regular basis

- Identifying and comparing key players at Global Coffee's competitors with those at Global Coffee

- Defining the future of communications inside Global Coffee

THE BOTTOM LINE

The ARL approach produced results at different levels. On the business side, overall the company was able to realize between US$3 million and US$4 million in actual savings and/or earnings from the various NLP project solutions. The executive team estimated that millions more were saved or earned from organizational efficiencies, customer satisfaction, supplier satisfaction, and employee satisfaction resulting from more efficient organizational processes, better-quality service, and more effective leaders and managers.

On the organizational level, a real culture shift took place. Throughout this entire process, Learning Coaches were working with the executive team and role-modeling the desired team behaviors they were advocating across the company.

On a more personal level, several NLP graduates had a transformational experience. They were more accepting of themselves and their strengths, less judgmental, more curious, better listeners, better team leaders, and more appreciative managers. They took their lessons and new behaviors to their functional teams and site teams, applying ARL principles, concepts, and tools. As a consequence, their own teams and organizations became higher-performing entities. The collective effect across this group of sixty created a strong ripple of organizational change across the entire company.

The changes were so profound that the HR department received a national award for developing Global Coffee's competitive advantage with the NLP. At about the same time, Global Coffee's mother company decided to get out of the coffee business. The board of directors wanted to focus on its core business, which was not coffee. However, they were able to get a premium price for Global Coffee. Much of the credit was due to Global Coffee's flexibility, leadership depth, organizational effectiveness, customer loyalty, and global competitiveness.

And while the company changed one more time as it entered into another merger, individuals took with them new ways of thinking, doing, and being. As one NLP graduate put it: "We moved from 'human doings' to 'human beings.'" Not a bad outcome!

◀ ARL ELEMENTS HIGHLIGHTED IN THIS STORY ▶

In this chapter, we introduced nine of the sixteen key learning elements that constitute the core of ARL. More elements will be highlighted in the stories that follow.

We have noted alongside the text some of the ARL elements that were implemented through different tools or processes. Below are descriptions of each element highlighted in the story and its application in the particular case. See chapter 10 for an in-depth discussion of the ARL elements.

▶ **Element: Ownership of the Learning**

Operational description: To involve the learner in setting learning goals and recommending contents.

What the ARL team did: Participants' voices were collected through the culture survey. The planning team involved and engaged the key stakeholders throughout the design process and during the program.

▶ **Element: Balancing Task and Learning**

Operational description: To give equal attention to the progress on the task (the content) and to the learning (the process).

What the ARL team did: The work on real projects became the arena for learning the skills and competencies and at the same time for developing new perspectives, attitudes, and behaviors.

▶ **Element: Just-in-Time Intervention**

Operational description: To introduce concepts, tools, questions, and interventions just when they are needed.

What the ARL team did: We looked for learning opportunities during the team's project work and contracted the right to stop work on the task and focus on the many team processes.

▶ **Element: Appreciative Approach**

Operational description: To promote an atmosphere of mutual recognition and acceptance, fostering empowerment.

What the ARL team did: We consciously looked for what was working well and emphasized this.

▶ **Element: Guided Reflection**

Operational description: To direct learners toward reflection.

What the ARL team did: We periodically provided opportunities for guided reflection using a process called Stop, Reflect, Write, Report, which gives participants the opportunity to think about what they are learning, clarify any areas of confusion, and share their insights with the group.

▶ **Element: Safe Environment**

Operational description: To create a safe environment that encourages learners to speak up and try out behaviors.

What the ARL team did: The mere presence of a Learning Coach often helped create a safe environment. We also introduced simple processes that contributed to a safe environment, such as facilitating a team's creation of norms.

▶ **Element: Unfamiliar Environments**

Operational description: To expose learners to unfamiliar situations that generate reflection and uncover their own mental maps and models.

What the ARL team did: Teams were created with an eye to maximizing diversity of all kinds—function, nationality, gender, age, and the like. Since no team member was assigned to a challenge related to his or her area of expertise, all team members were forced to work without the influence of "expert power" that sometimes inhibits creativity.

▶ **Element: Sequenced Learning**

Operational description: To sequence modules or meetings over a period of time so that learners can try out what they have learned in their home settings. Then, when they return to the learning group, they can exchange lessons and receive feedback on coaching before once again going back to their home settings.

What the ARL team did: Through a four-module design, we gave participants time to go back and try out some of what they had learned. They came back after several weeks to share their successes as well as the difficulties they had encountered and get support, coaching, and tips on how to continually move forward.

◀ **ARL ELEMENTS HIGHLIGHTED IN THIS STORY** cont'd ▶

▶ **Element: Learning Coach**

Operational description: A Learning Coach fills multiple roles: designing learning programs; helping individuals and teams reflect on their experiences; introducing tools and concepts, just in time; asking questions for reflections; challenging individuals and teams in a caring manner; and creating a safe environment for learning.

What the ARL team did: One coach was assigned to every project team. Each coach also provided one-on-one support throughout the program.

SUMMING UP

In this chapter, we introduced nine of the sixteen elements that constitute the core of ARL. More elements are highlighted in chapter 3.

A Leadership Transition

Thomas was the managing director of the Thai office of a multi-national corporation, a position he had successfully held for three years. Now he was preparing for a new challenge in another Far Eastern country, a position to which he had been promoted.

Thomas wanted to support the executive team in its transition to the next leader. He was also interested in extracting learnings from the experience that he could use in his next assignment and which the team would find valuable, too. All the members of his executive team were Thai, with a long history in the organization, and had become a cohesive group. They had seen different leaders assigned to that position and appeared sanguine and ready to work with the next one.

Thomas was particularly concerned because the new executive was a very straight-talking person, and the team had a notably different approach to communication. In his three years in the position, Thomas, of U.S. origin, had faced numerous challenges with the cultural aspects of the local organization. He decided to get help and contacted us.

THE LAND OF SMILES

"This is the land of smiles," Thomas said. "You will notice it wherever you go. People smile at you, whether they know you or not, and you may not understand why. The reason is that there are twelve different smiles—something Westerners can hardly comprehend. The downside for Westerners," he continued, "is that we can never be really sure what the smile might mean or imply, or what the person is truly thinking or feeling."

After arriving in Thailand, Thomas quickly realized that it was more important to his executives to give him good news than to present tough facts. One of the Thais' most important values is *krengjai,* meaning "not to cause discomfort to the other." They valued social harmony to such an extent that they carefully avoided conflict and discussions. This also eliminated what might have been valuable conversations about differing points of view. In addition, Thai culture is extremely respectful of hierarchies and seniority and pays special attention to saving face—not only for themselves, but especially for seniors and authorities. He said that if Thais were to report difficulties to him, it would be seen as exposing him to an unpleasant situation in which he might lose face. And in the Thai culture, this is simply unacceptable.

During his stay in Thailand, Thomas invested time and energy in repeatedly telling his team his expectations and his preferred communication style as a sensitive man who liked to listen to others and valued honesty and openness; he was nonjudgmental but pragmatic. He looked for clear communications with his staff so that they could jointly reach the goals, supporting them where they needed it. In return, he expected them to share their thoughts, dilemmas, and difficulties with him rather than protect him.

After three years, he was still not sure that his words really were understood. The language gap was a clear challenge, as he had no understanding of Thai, which his team members used in their daily work together. But he wondered whether this was simply a linguistic hurdle or one comprising both language and culture.

PREPARING FOR A
SMOOTH TRANSITION

Now that Thomas was leaving, he was worried that the incoming leader would experience the same difficulties. He wanted to help both parties have a smoother integration. Moreover, he was interested in extracting any possible lessons from this experience. "I wish they could talk to me openly, give me real feedback," Thomas said. "It would be so useful for my own professional development to be able to try out different approaches in my next assignment, which will be in another Asian culture. But asking for feedback is simply an impossible dream in this culture. It just won't happen. I wish I could tell them how it felt for me at the beginning," he continued, "and what they could do differently with the new leader. I wish they could accept that they don't have to go through the same process; we could all learn."

The solution was a jointly designed event in which all participants could reflect, extract lessons, give feedback to one another, express their thoughts, feelings, and concerns, and explore approaches to try out with the next leader. To prepare for the meeting, we asked Thomas what outcomes he wished for, from a professional perspective and from personal, team, organizational, and business sides. As he described the relationship with his team, we highlighted the fact that many of his opinions sounded like assumptions, supported by three years of challenging interactions with a different culture.

A SUCCESSFUL EVENT

Thomas communicated to his team that we had been invited in to support him and them during a one-day session as they considered together how best to manage the leadership transition.

The meeting started with Thomas leading introductions and presenting an outline of his intent and the objectives. He ex-

---

Ownership of the Learning

Five Dimensions System

Letting Thomas set the outcomes and expectations gave him ownership of the learning that would emerge from the meeting. To ensure lasting results, the work was based on the Five Dimensions System, a learning system that considers and measures outcomes for (1) the company or business, (2) the organization as a whole, (3) the specific team, (4) individuals' professional competencies, and (5) individuals' personal attitudes and mindsets.

Learning Coach

In this event, we acted as Learning Coaches, on hand to set the appropriate stage for the task and learning.

Ownership of the Learning

Setting expectations and reading them out loud was the participants' first step toward accepting some ownership of the process and influencing session outcomes.

Safe Environment Learning and Personality Styles

By setting norms that they wanted respected during the session, the team members established a safe environment in which to accomplish this unfamiliar task of feedback. Further, writing instead of proclaiming those norms kept the shyest team members in (or at least near) their comfort zones.

plained that our role as outside consultants was to help him and the team work on the task and extract lessons at the same time. We also would support all members of the group as they rode out some rough water in a very new cross-cultural experience.

As coaches, we shared the agenda and asked everyone to take a moment to reflect silently and write down his or her expectations for the meeting. We explained that we had chosen that process in order to hear everyone's expectations and collect them in writing as visual guidance for the group. This meeting had to serve everyone, we indicated, and we would try to include their individual expectations in the design. Then we asked each person to read his or her expectation out loud. We feared that the expectations would be very general and noncommittal; instead, they seemed sincere, personal, and concrete.

Next, we introduced the process of setting norms and stated the rationale for the procedure. We invited everyone in the room to write down one norm that we should respect during the session, based on their experiences of what had helped in other meetings. The shyest team members welcomed the process of silent writing and seemed to enjoy what was for them an unaccustomed setting.

Norms included no judging, freedom to speak or to remain silent, sharing thoughts or feelings, and careful listening for the deeper meaning. After the norms were set, Thomas explained to his team his sincere need to learn from them their view of his performance as their leader. Following our preparatory coaching conversations, we had agreed that this request for feedback would be best positioned as a "good-bye gift." We speculated that in a culture that places so much value on pleasing, a gift would be the best way to reframe feedback.

"I am taking an important step in my career," Thomas stated. "I will be facing another culture, different from this one and from those I have experienced before. I think you could help me in this new challenge by sharing with me your advice about what I should continue doing and what I should try to do differently in the new context. You have lived through these three years; you are in the best position to give me that good-bye gift." He, in turn, offered a similar "gift" from his perspective—one that could help them in their integration with the next leader.

After this introduction, we took over the facilitation role. We invited Thomas to go to the room next door and gave him and the team a similar assignment.

Team members had to begin with an individual reflection on what they would recommend Thomas continue to do in his next job, that is, what in their opinion was effective behavior, and also what they thought he might consider changing or trying out. Then they would share their thoughts and record a summary on a flip-chart. Team members also had to decide what to pass along to Thomas and who would be the spokesperson. After giving the instructions, we left the room so they would feel more comfortable and discuss the task in their own language.

Thomas had a similar task. He had to reflect on what they as a team should continue doing with the new leader and what they might consider doing differently.

After a while, both parties were ready and visibly excited about the exchange. We asked them what they liked, and they commented on the idea of the "gift" and also the notion that past experience could be seen as a lesson for the future. We added that this resonated with the value that many Asian peoples ascribe to the wisdom of experience; elders have something to transfer to younger people because they have acquired more wisdom through experience. This is comparable to what we in our Western practice use as lessons from the past.

To honor the respect for hierarchy in Thailand, and also to lower anxiety by proceeding in a way that was more comfortable for the participants (the whole feedback process was, after all, a

Appreciative Approach

Although ARL coaches frequently ask participants to go against their traditions and habits, coaches must still show that they respect these past traditions and the culture. By positioning the session as "gifts" from one party to the other, we showed our appreciation of the Thai culture.

Guided Reflection

We set the parameters of the reflection and then left the team and Thomas alone to reflect on those issues—and, in the case of team members, to share individual reflections with one another.

One-on-One Coaching Support

Safe Environment

Since the whole feedback process was so unfamiliar and a bit uncomfortable, we did everything possible to add familiar or comfortable components to the environment in which the process was taking place. The fishbowl setting—Thomas speaking uninterrupted as if the others were not listening, and the team spokesperson doing likewise—was one such component.

Guided Reflection

Just-in-Time Intervention

Safe Environment

Holistic Involvement of the Individual

The reflection and dialogue session brought together many key elements of the ARL approach. Reflection was the core goal. Questions from us and from participants guided the reflective conversation. Setting norms for the dialogue contributed to the safeness of the

distinct novelty in the Thai culture), we suggested that Thomas speak first. We had agreed on this strategy during our planning conversations.

We used a "fishbowl" setting. Thomas sat with the two of us in the center of a circle and shared his reflections out loud, pretending no one else was in the room. This also helped members of the team lower their anxiety and listen better. His team members sat silently in the circle until he finished. Then we invited them to ask him questions, but at this time for points of clarification only.

Next, it was the team's turn. In a sign of respect for seniority, team members had selected the oldest among them as their spokesperson. We used the same fishbowl format: The spokesperson had a conversation with us, seated in the center, while Thomas listened in the outer circle, taking notes on the issues that he wanted to ask about later.

We ended with a reflection and dialogue session, in which individuals are given some minutes to collect their thoughts in silence on a specific question prior to expressing themselves in dialogue. Everyone sat in a circle and had a conversation about the question "What have we learned from this experience, and how do we feel?" This exercise introduced a new way of communication to the executive team: They had never taken silent time for reflection in the work setting, nor were they used to extracting lessons from a regular meeting. Sitting in a circle without a table in front of them was also something new and strange, but the safety net provided by the norms of the dialogue helped calm the anxiety.

Team members were actively engaged and showed great enthusiasm for and excitement about this novel experience. They commented on the honor of being able to give such a gift to their leader, and we reflected on the different ways of giving feedback. They discovered that feedback could be a positive, constructive process, highlighting what the person did well and converting any critical feedback into caring suggestions and advice. Everyone spoke in that session; everyone's honest voice was heard. Thoughts, personal reflections, impressions, and feelings were expressed. One team member wondered how many other opportunities there might be for reviewing assumptions people have about one another or for giving feedback in a caring, respectful, and useful way. This was a real breakthrough that they all clearly enjoyed.

RESULTS OF
THE INTERVENTION

This one-day event had an interesting impact. From the leader's perspective, it challenged his assumptions; he realized that taking a risk and trying something different, even at the closing stage of this particular team, had been a powerful initiative. He also received some valuable feedback from the team members; he heard a few recommendations he had never expected that would be of great value in his next leadership assignment.

Thomas realized that the advice came at the cost of not having had "perfect" communication with team members during his three years on the job, because he had not been able to get candid feedback from them, bound as they were by their cultural traditions. But at least now the feedback was indeed a gift that would convert a challenging experience into constructive learning for the future. By sharing his perspective and feedback with them, he was able to expand their thinking on how they had contributed in the past to the cross-cultural misunderstandings.

Both parties were suddenly able to recognize that it was a complex challenge; there was no right/wrong, good/bad, appropriate/inappropriate duality. It was an experience of two different

(cont'd)

setting. Individuals were free to be holistically involved, having the choice to speak about feelings or to share rational or spiritual thoughts.

Balancing Task and Learning

Learning Exchange

Linking

The entire session was a successful balance of task (giving and receiving feedback) and learning (reflecting on and learning from that feedback). The session allowed the team and Thomas to share their perspectives, the heart of the Learning Exchange element. And it gave the team the opportunity to bring the learnings from that day and apply them to different situations, the Linking element.

Unfamiliar Environments Feedback

This case highlights the power of unfamiliar environments—asking the Thai executives to participate in a one-day feedback session—to get participants out of their comfort zones and create some real learning and the instructional power of feedback itself.

Linking

Because Thomas was leaving, the real goal of the session was to help the team and Thomas apply their learning to the situations each would face in the future—to link what they learned that day to other contexts.

Sequenced Learning

(The missing element)

worldviews, values, traditions—even two different languages, although not only in the linguistic sense. But as they had lived together through these years, they had jointly constructed a relationship that was mutually influencing.

We made sure to give team members enough time to process this experience fully—to internalize what had just happened and what had happened in the past—so that they all could understand its meaning for each of them personally and extract conclusions. This guided them in considering other circumstances under which these same dynamics might occur, how they had each contributed to the situation, and what they might do differently in the future.

Given their extremely satisfactory experience, the Thai team members were confident that there could be some ways in which upward communicating could remain respectful yet be candid. This was an important reflection, for not only their present but also their future cross-cultural relationships, including but not limited to those they would have with the incoming leader. For Thomas, it highlighted both the power of self-fulfilling prophecies and the opportunities available to influence an unhappy situation, by taking risks and by refusing to accept that even strong traditions are immutable. As he came to the end of his Thailand chapter, he recognized that each ending serves as the preface for a new beginning.

Usually, all of the ARL elements are part of an intervention. However, this intervention did not use the ARL element Sequenced Learning—applying and reinforcing the original learning from the one-day session. Under normal circumstances, we would have facilitated one or two more meetings with the group in order to see how group members tried to apply their learning and new perspectives and what results or difficulties they encountered, and to support them in addressing those challenges. In this case, it was not possible to continue the process, which would have required meeting with the team and the incoming leader, including the new leader in this shared know-how, following up in the application of lessons learned with Thomas, using the new approach for giving and receiving feedback, reflecting, and exchanging lessons. Thomas, however, was able to apply some of the recommendations and learning in his new position, which resulted in an extraordinarily successful assignment.

THE CULTURAL CHALLENGE

This story illustrates the application of Western ARL elements in a one-day event with a small intact team steeped in a culture of traditional Eastern values. We had surmised, and events confirmed, that the ARL elements provided the flexibility and room to help the team adapt to a different environment. Having the right cultural awareness and sensitivity is key, so that the Learning Coach is able to understand the areas of potential conflict. It is not axiomatic that Western OD methodologies translate to all cultures, but our central belief is that suggestions have to be sensitively presented, in full acknowledgment that we are asking others to try a different behavior. We need to be creative when designing sessions that are adapted to and respectful of the participants' values. At the same time, a dose of challenge is necessary, as the event is meant to take them out of their comfort zones. In this case, by framing the exercise in the context of a cultural tradition of gift giving, the session permitted the team to engage in new behaviors, and for a powerful good.

◀ **ARL ELEMENTS HIGHLIGHTED IN THIS STORY** ▶

Following our just-in-time process highlights, we have again marked several ARL elements alongside the story. Nine were introduced in chapter 2. The seven that follow are new; they complete the list of sixteen elements that constitute the core of ARL.

▶ **Element: Five Dimensions System**

Operational description: To generate lasting learning. We consider five dimensions in the design and delivery of any learning intervention: the problem or business challenge, the organization, the team, the professional competencies, and the personal attitudes or mind-sets.

What the ARL team did: We explored the possible outcomes in the five dimensions with the team leader and incorporated them into the design. We worked to develop feedback-giving skills (*professional* dimension) and introduced a process for it, but we also explored the *personal* values and beliefs that had to accompany the technique. We worked with the group to see how they would use it within their *team* and with others, and we guided them in exploring the *business* benefit of adopting the new practice. We tried to challenge the organizational norm of avoiding candid feedback.

▶ **Element: Learning and Personality Styles**

Operational description: When designing learning activities, to accommodate the preferences of all learners in terms of learning and personality styles and also challenge them so that they are working inside and outside their comfort zones.

What the ARL team did: We paid attention to the different personality and learning styles in designing and facilitating the event. We framed each activity, explaining why we were doing it, what we would do, how we would do it, and what the implications would be for participants, so as to include the different learning preferences. We made learning points both in writing and orally, alternating them in order to balance the needs of introverts and extraverts. The free brainstorming session catered to the divergent thinkers, and structured elements such as flip-charts, next steps, and summaries supported the need for closure of the convergent thinkers.

▶ **Element: One-on-One Coaching Support**

Operational description: To support learners in an individual way.

What the ARL team did: We provided individual support mainly for the team leader and at a more moderate level for some of the participants, when we had brief supportive exchanges during the breaks.

▶ **Element: Holistic Involvement of the Individual**

Operational description: To create opportunities for learners to express themselves intellectually, emotionally, and spiritually.

What the ARL team did: Typically, an introduction exercise with an intact team tends to center on participants stating their name and role—a shallow formula of little value. We invited them to introduce themselves in a broader way, saying something about themselves that the others in the room, with whom they had worked for years, didn't know. By doing this, the introductions achieved a deeper level of understanding—not just a formality for the visiting coaches, but an activity that connected the team members in a new way. They were able to share information of their choosing, and they all elected to mention something from their personal lives. They used the opportunity to have a more integral presence, to present themselves as more than executives in charge of a certain function. Furthermore, we opened the possibility of sharing feelings and thoughts during the dialogue session, which several participants welcomed and used.

▶ **Element: Learning Exchange**

Operational description: To generate situations in which learners exchange their perspectives in order to enrich, multiply, and expand their exposure to new learnings.

What the ARL team did: When group members worked without coaches, they were able to begin an exchange of perspectives and learnings. Also, through dialogue, participants were able to hear what other team members had learned as well as contribute to the final debrief of the event.

▶ **Element: Linking**

Operational description: To transfer the learning to other scenarios so that the individual is encouraged to adapt and apply it, to extract concepts and conclusions at a higher level of abstraction.

What the ARL team did: During the dialogue and the debrief, we explicitly asked team members to think of opportunities for using the processes they had experienced that day and describe how they would do it. We also connected the tools that were introduced to other situations in which they could be used.

▶ **Element: Feedback**

Operational description: To provide opportunities for giving and receiving feedback as a way to build cause–effect connections within one's own behavior, thus increasing self-awareness.

What the ARL team did: In this case, the main focus of the event was on introducing feedback.

◀ **PREVIOUSLY INTRODUCED ELEMENTS** ▶

For the following elements, introduced in chapter 2, we describe in detail how they were applied in the given context. While the elements remain the same in any context, the way they are applied varies and is open to the creativity of the coach.

▶ **Element: Ownership of the Learning**

What the ARL team did: The leader's expectations were collected in the co-design session, and the participants' voices were collected through an expectations-sharing exercise. We also set norms to aid in shaping the meeting and the agreed behaviors of all members.

▶ **Element: Learning Coach**

What the ARL team did: We contracted with the leader regarding both his and our roles, designed the event, facilitated the process, and ensured that the event would flow in a supportive and challenging atmosphere.

▶ **Element: Safe Environment**

What the ARL team did: We as coaches ran a session to set the norms, paid special attention to cultural sensitivities during both the planning and the event, and introduced the fishbowl process, which made the feedback exchange more comfortable. Our presence worked as a guarantor of a protected environment.

▶ **Element: Appreciative Approach**

What the ARL team did: We positioned the feedback as a good-bye gift, thereby creating a framework for team members to "permit" themselves to behave in a nontraditional manner.

▶ **Element: Guided Reflection**

What the ARL team did: We designed and facilitated segments in which we invited participants to stop, reflect, and review their lessons learned.

▶ **Element: Just-in-Time Intervention**

What the ARL team did: The feedback process was actually a just-in-time intervention, as it was a highly relevant topic for the group at that point. In addition, we introduced some tools and processes for reflection, for reporting, for appointing, and for making decisions.

▶ **Element: Balancing Task and Learning**

What the ARL team did: The agenda task, to give and receive feedback, was balanced with segments to reflect and extract lessons by choosing a learning question for the dialogue session and for the debrief.

▶ **Element: Unfamiliar Environments**

What the ARL team did: Although Thomas and his team members knew one another well, Thomas experienced the unfamiliar setting through taking the risk of such an event at the closure of his role in Thailand. For the executive team, several components of the event were extremely unfamiliar: sitting in a circle, reflecting in silence, giving and receiving candid feedback, and writing before talking.

SUMMING UP

In chapters 2 and 3, we have introduced all sixteen ARL elements:

- Appreciative Approach
- Balancing Task and Learning
- Feedback
- Five Dimensions System
- Guided Reflection
- Holistic Involvement of the Individual
- Just-in-Time Intervention
- Learning and Personality Styles
- Learning Coach
- Learning Exchange
- Linking
- One-on-One Coaching Support

- Ownership of the Learning
- Safe Environment
- Sequenced Learning
- Unfamiliar Environments

The ways in which the elements were applied varied in response to the context, the contents, and the outcomes targeted. And there is more to discover.

Let us take you to the next stop on the journey.

CHAPTER 4

ARL in Education

The previous stops on our journey have taken you to corporate environments. We want to invite you now to another setting, that of education.

We begin with an extremely problematic urban school in the United States that needed to learn how to change. We then take you to South America, where ARL elements guided the teaching of a master's course in a business school. Finally, we return to the United States and attend a program for school leaders who wanted to learn about leadership and learning.

Since the sixteen ARL elements have already been introduced and defined, we simply "boxed" them throughout the text and skipped the descriptions at the end of the chapter.

DEVELOPING A LOCAL SCHOOL
Storyteller: Ernie

Several years ago, I made a presentation to a number of principals in an urban school district on an approach designed to help turn around failing schools. We were looking for schools where the

Unfamiliar Environments

principals were interested in trying out an innovative approach to school governance called Local School Development, or Local D.

The acronym caught people's attention and roused their curiosity. Our tagline then was "Local D: Giving a voice to those who have a stake." At the end of the presentation, Ray, a strong, gruff-looking principal, raised his hand and said, "Whatever Local D is, I'm willing to give it a try. I've tried everything else, and nothing has worked!"

Ray, an African American, was big, imposing, and opinionated, yet he had a caring heart under his tough exterior. Unfortunately, his caring side seldom showed, as he felt he needed to appear strong. He and Bob, the Irish local school-union representative who was big, imposing, and opinionated as well, did not see eye to eye. In fact, their disagreements were even rumored to have become physical at one point. So the teachers' loyalties were split between Ray and Bob, mostly along racial lines.

The parents were not organized and had no voice. There was no student organization either. The community had given up on the school.

The physical status of the school was deplorable. There were more broken than unbroken windows in the building, and only a handful of doors had doorknobs, as the others had been kicked off by the students. The district superintendent was withholding funds for windows and doorknobs until the school got its act together. In violation of the fire code, the custodian had chained all the doors but the main door in order to keep intruders out. He had also, for the students' protection, removed the doors to the lavatories, since many muggings took place there. He had also removed all bulletin boards from the interior hallways because students routinely set them on fire. The top floor was barricaded because it had not been renovated after students had set it on fire.

The school was notorious across the city's entire public school system. It had one of the highest teacher and student assault rates in the city, and it was in the bottom 5 percent in math and reading scores. Moreover, it had one of the highest student and teacher absentee rates. The neighborhood was predominantly African American and Hispanic, and many of the families were headed by single parents.

When classes were in session, there were frequently more students in the hallways than in the classrooms. The teachers' lounge had been vandalized, so teachers tended to cluster in the teachers' cafeteria when they had a free period. The cloud of marijuana smoke in the stairwells was thick enough to make people high if they lingered there too long. This was definitely not a cathedral of learning.

The Discovery Phase

My first step was to do a little firsthand "discovery" work. I spent a week interviewing all of the various constituencies: administrators (Ray, his three assistant principals, and the dean of students); teachers, including the head of the union; any parents I could find; the support staff, including the custodian; students; and a few community representatives from the police precinct, the local community college, and the community board.

During the interview process, I was once surrounded in the hallway by a gang of students and their dog during class time and threatened with what could have been a knife or a gun hidden under the gang leader's shirt. Fortunately, I was able to turn this confrontation into a productive interview by inviting these students to answer some of the questions I had been asking other students. It was certainly my most memorable interview in the discovery process.

All in all, we got the same basic message: Learning isn't taking place, there is very little teaching going on, the school isn't safe for anyone, everyone is blaming everyone else for the school's failure, no one is working together, and no one is happy. We had a challenge on our hands. These were the circumstances I discovered when I began our partnership with Ray to see if Local D could make a difference.

Ownership of the Learning

The Plan

When I presented our basic findings to Ray, his assistant principals, and his dean of students, they were not surprised and wanted to know what I planned on doing. I laid out our strategy, which was pretty simple: We had to give those who have a stake in this school a legitimate voice if we expect the school to become anything close to an arena for learning. In practical terms, this meant sharing decision-making power with teachers, parents, students, support staff, and community representatives. After a somber moment of reflection, they agreed that they had nothing to lose, as they had tried everything else. I spent some time coaching Ray on his new role as ambassador for the creation of a learning environment and on his strategy for empowering a constituency-based planning team with representatives from all the key stakeholders mentioned above.

One-on-One Coaching Support

Ownership of the Learning

His first task was to help the parents and students get organized so that they, in turn, could have a representative voice in this new power-sharing process. That took a couple of months. In the meantime, Ray met with the teachers and let them know that he really needed their help and wanted them to select a couple of teachers who would be willing to join this team-in-formation. He also met with the various community groups and asked for their help. Ray, to his great surprise, quickly discovered that asking for help was like magic. Everyone was willing to give some time, energy, and ideas.

The team had two teachers, two parents, two students, one assistant principal, the dean of students (who was elected as the team chairperson), and two community representatives, one from a community-based neighborhood organization and the other from the local community college. The parent organization, teacher organization, and student organization each selected two representatives. I served as their coach, supporting them first in becoming a team and then with their planning process as they brought their dreams to fruition. I worked closely with the chairperson, Rose, an energetic and caring African American woman who was respected and trusted by everyone in the school, including Ray. Her role was very instrumental in getting the team to work together.

Once the team was selected and assembled, we suggested that Ray basically commission the team by stating its mandate and clarifying the limits of its decision-making authority so that he wouldn't need to veto recommendations that were outside its jurisdiction. Virtually everything, except teacher appraisals and changing the curriculum, were within the limits. Any decisions team members made would become recommendations that required Ray's confirmation. I also suggested that Ray join the team only when its members needed his input or when he needed to make a special request or offer—at least for the time being. Without his presence, which could be rather intimidating, they would be able to become a team and speak more freely.

Safe Environment

I became Ray's coach and the team's coach. I participated in all team meetings and worked closely with the team chairperson as well. I was able to provide just-in-time feedback, questions, concepts, and tools. My goal, in essence, was to help the team believe in itself and maximize its performance.

One-on-One Coaching Support

The Action

The team took its job seriously and met weekly. At my suggestion, team members spent three days at an outdoor environmental education center, where they got to know one another better, did some team building using outdoor exercises, refined their own mission, created a future vision, contracted roles and team norms, and began developing their change plan for the school.

Holistic Involvement of the Individual

Safe Environment

Ownership of the Learning

I was there to support them as a facilitator and a coach in getting the most out of those three days away. I encouraged them to dream together as a team and to accept that they were limited only by their imaginations.

Learning Coach

The team emerged from the retreat with a list of creative, ambitious ideas. Ray approved every one of them, and within a few months the brainstorming ideas were becoming reality. One of the most effective and exciting decisions team members made at their meeting was to create an after-school center, because the school basically closed down at 3:00 P.M., and the kids had nowhere to go and nothing to do except get into trouble.

In just a few weeks, the planning team had converted this dream into a vibrant program with a wide variety of offerings. A teacher and a parent on the team volunteered to take the lead organizing role in setting up schedules, contracting roles and responsibilities, and ensuring that resources were available. They even got the custodian's support in providing the necessary cleanup. The after-school center became a focus of energy and a magnet for kids and teachers. Almost everyone got involved and contributed ideas and talent. Teachers, students, administrators, parents, and community volunteers led a range of activities including tennis, guitar lessons, poetry, basketball, singing, dance, theater, painting, and magic.

Students couldn't wait for school to end so they could participate in or lead an activity. And instead of punching out at 3:00 P.M. sharp and heading home, many teachers were staying on and volunteering their time to conduct or participate in activities. The school received a small grant from a foundation to pay for some of the supplies, but the participants themselves supplied the lion's share. As the team became more and more skilled and confident in making decisions and plans, the school, in turn, was becoming an exciting place to be.

The superintendent invested in doorknobs and windows. The custodian reinstalled the bulletin boards. He also replaced hundreds of missing tiles in the bathrooms and put the doors back on. The parents donated time and money to renovate the fourth floor and also made curtains for the windows. The students established their own hall monitoring system and were able to reduce the number of kids in the hallways during class time from several hundred to almost zero.

Ray was thrilled with the turnaround at the school and was smiling more than he was frowning. He didn't veto one recom-

Safe Environment Ownership of the Learning

Holistic Involvement of the Individual

Appreciative Approach

mendation that the team brought to him. Although the central union initially complained that the teachers were volunteering their time without pay to lead activities in the after-school center, it later changed its tune and, in a newspaper article, praised the efforts of teachers who were willing to go the extra mile for the good of the kids, citing the school as an example.

The school gained news media coverage of the dramatic change. Within eighteen months, it had become known for its innovation and turnaround. Teachers became curious about learning new ways of teaching. Ray and his team became coaches instead of disciplinarians. Students were happier and more engaged in learning. Reading and math scores increased; assault and absenteeism decreased. The school was becoming a safer, fun, and exciting place to teach and learn. Was it perfect? No. Planning team members felt that their task of turning the school around was still in the beginning stages. They still had dreams and plans, such as becoming the number one school in reading and math scores in the district. Parents were still concerned about their children's safety, so there was a perception problem that the school needed to overcome. Some teachers were still skeptical, fearing that this was just another fad that would fade away. However, the planning team was experienced and confident and had the skills to continue to dream, plan, and act. And the greater school community was committed to the school's success. The school was no longer on its own.

After several years, the central board of education was able to formally institutionalize the planning team concept that Ray and another fifty junior high school and elementary school principals had successfully implemented. Ray and his fellow principals had paved the way for this democratic change and revolutionary way of operating.

Ripple Effects

Several months after the school had turned the corner, another school, which had inherited the mantle as the most notorious high school in the city, faced a crisis. A group of students had picked up the principal, carried him outside, placed him on the sidewalk, and told him they didn't want to see him in the school again. So the chancellor picked up the phone and called Ray, saying, "Ray, I've got another challenge for you!" Ray, in turn, called us, saying, "Ernie, guess what? We have another school."

And so we jointly took the same concept to this new school, where we followed a very similar process. We set up a constituency-based planning team that received support in speaking up and creating a shared vision for the school. The process became an effective means for Ray to establish a healthy "contract" with parents, teachers, students, and other school administrators. He had discovered that he wasn't the only one who wanted to make a difference. He was able to apply his recent lessons of power sharing and delegating authority in order to empower others. He discovered that power is not a finite entity; the more one shares, the more there is to share.

Summary

When Ray accepted the unusual challenge of participating in the Local D intervention, he showed that he was ready for change and willing to review his own mental models about leading and teamwork. The time was right; the Local D offer came as a just-in-time intervention. Ray discovered the power of the words *help* and *thank you* and the importance of creating an appreciative environment. By involving the stakeholders and giving them a voice, we created the path for progressive ownership, which was crucial for the results. Everyone realized the power of working together, exchanging ideas, and thinking together. People learned how important it was to create a safe environment (physically, intellectually, and emotionally) as the foundation for teaching and learning. They all discovered how much knowledge they had in themselves as they came up with their own solutions to their many challenges. And they came to appreciate the value of a Learning Coach who was there to support them along the way—not only in making the changes their school needed but also in understanding how they made those changes by sharing leadership and focusing on learning. The planning team became a model of a learning organization and an inspiration to the rest of the school. Every constituency believed that it was important and had played a significant role in making this change happen. They could never have made these changes individually, but they did it together, proving an age-old adage: Together we stand, divided we fall.

CHANGING THE APPROACH TO TEACHING
Storyteller: Isabel

A few years ago, I was invited to teach a course on change management with a colleague as part of the Master's in Human Resources program at a South American university. The students were in their mid-thirties and were employed full-time, so they attended classes in the evenings.

The Intent

As we prepared the syllabus, I reflected on the outcomes I would like for students who took the course. What did I want to achieve? I determined that, at the end of the course, I would want students to have explored the characteristics of change, the factors that make it challenging, the enablers and blockers, and the key aspects that require attention when designing or implementing change processes. I wanted them to be able to read materials that could contribute to and expand their understanding. I wanted them to have the opportunity to identify and review their assumptions about change, to explore their own roles, both current and potential, in influencing change. I wanted them to find answers to their questions about change. And I wanted them to come up with a tangible product resulting from the application of their learning.

My colleague agreed to the outcomes, following my suggestions to craft the course in line with the ARL approach, which was new to him at that time.

The Kickoff

In the first session, in order to guide the introduction process, we asked the students what they wanted to know about us. This was an unusual start, which caused uncertainty and baffled smiles.

Unfamiliar Environments

After the introductions, we explained that the course would be successful only if it met their expectations, so we wanted to give them a moment to collect their thoughts and write down their expectations, both in terms of content and from us as instructors. This was the second puzzling request, for the common assumption was that students attend classes to learn from expert professors who know best what students need to know and how to teach it. More than an assumption, we knew this was part of the educational culture, and we were aware that we were deliberately challenging that belief.

Ownership of the Learning

After some murmurs, a student spoke up and said, "Professor, we cannot tell you what we want you to teach because we don't know the subject!" We were happy to hear that comment, because it gave us the opportunity to explain that we were asking them simply to write down what aroused their curiosity or intrigued them about change, what questions they would like to have answered during the course.

Ownership of the Learning

Guided Reflection

This provided some relief, and they all began to write in their notebooks. After a while, we asked them to share their questions and filled the board with their input.

Not surprisingly, when we asked what they expected from us, and what type of approach or roles they wanted, there was another puzzled and nervous silence. We repeated that they were our clients who paid our salaries, and it was not unreasonable to ask what they expected from us so that we could better serve them. They thought this was very comic, and the room exploded in laughter, which helped relieve the tension our unusual approach was creating.

Finally, some students spoke up and said things like "not pure lectures," "real cases," "discussions, not monologues by you," "connecting it with our work," "something useful," "hearing your experience with real situations." We took notes and agreed to those expectations. We were somewhat surprised by how quickly a traditional educational setting and stance could turn around, with the students going from a passive to an active, participative mode.

We ended the first session by asking them to collectively set the norms for working together during the semester. At that point, the energy was high, and everyone was enjoying the strange experience, wondering, "What's next?" With less resistance than we'd experienced with the previous requests, we were able to jointly identify our rules of the game. The students indicated that we, the teachers, should come well prepared, be on time, and end the class on time. We should be willing to provide support and feedback. They offered to arrive on time, read what was required for each session, and participate in the class discussions.

Safe Environment

A Few Weeks Later

We organized the course around change initiatives that they, the students, identified for us to work on. Students each found an organizational challenge from their work settings, where they had the opportunity to analyze and implement a change. For our part, we organized the readings around those real challenges. During each class, we discussed readings about one topic related to the course and explored how the concepts applied to their individual cases; they then incorporated their reflections into their papers for the next class. We agreed on three intermediate submissions of their papers, so that they could get our more detailed feedback and correct and modify their work for their final submissions.

The plan was that, at the end of the semester, they would have final papers incorporating lessons applied along the way. The theory was good, but a few weeks into the semester we had our first difficulties. Some students began to miss class, and those who attended were hiding behind one another to avoid participation.

They weren't reading the assigned texts, and when I asked for questions the readings had generated there was an uncomfortable silence and tension in the room. I shared my perception that they were not reading the assignments, based on the guilt I saw on their faces.

Ownership of the Learning

I explained that we had collectively agreed upon this process— using the classes for discussion—but if they didn't do the reading, there would not be much to discuss. One student spoke up and explained that the other teachers were much stricter and were asking for papers along with the reading, so the students were electing to complete assignments for teachers who were giving bad grades for not doing the assigned reading. I replied that this was all right and that although we had jointly agreed on this methodology, it often happens that we don't know if a process will work until we try it. Since this approach didn't seem to be working for them, we could modify it. Without resorting to disciplinary action or grades, we teachers were willing to adopt a lecturing approach if that would work better.

I will never forget the silence in the room. The students were absorbed in themselves, reflecting on what was going on, trying to make sense of it. Finally, one student said, "Professor, I don't think we should change the method we agreed upon. I think we just didn't live up to the norms. I think this is very strange, because we have had seventeen years of schooling under a different system. We learned to behave differently as students; all our lives we were rewarded for memorizing, for taking notes, for listening in silence without questioning expert teachers. I think we are just not used to this! But I think it's worth trying. Could you give us another chance, to see if we can do this? Because, after all, we asked for it."

The whole group burst out with comments of approval and support for his suggestions. We, as teachers, felt happy with this turn of events. We also were happy not to have to lecture, but most of all we thought that something important had just happened. Indeed, attendance was almost perfect for the rest of the semester; the students were enthusiastic and worked on their cases, using the readings as a supplement to their thinking; participation in class was very high; and students appreciated the feedback they received on their papers. Their final product was something useful, and they felt proud of it. We jointly set the criteria for grading and invited them to self-grade their papers, reserving our right to disagree. We were surprised to notice that they all graded themselves lower than what we thought they deserved. Their standards seemed to be higher than ours in the end.

Summary

I selected this story because I thought it was a good example of how the traditional educational system shapes our behaviors. These students were in their mid-thirties; as college graduates, they had an average of eight to ten years of work experience. They held junior management positions. They were used to being proactive in their working roles, but somehow, the moment they stepped into the classroom, they left their proactive behavior outside. They went back to their familiar "student" role, in which knowledge comes from the teacher and they take notes and absorb the instructor's expertise. Yet, when we pushed them to express their hopes, they mentioned participation, discussion, and real cases rather than lectures and theories.

This learning intervention was designed using the ARL elements: We intentionally pushed the students to accept ownership for their actions and learning; we used questions and their own answers as part of the course materials; we contributed our expertise and resources just in time, following the dynamics of both the discussions and their projects; we promoted exchange of lessons; we created a very unfamiliar yet safe environment; we introduced reflection and respected the diversity of learning styles. In terms of what Ron Heifetz calls "adaptive leadership," we used the crisis in the classroom as an example in order to learn about change.[7] I never mentioned ARL. We just tried it, and it made sense.

DESIGNING A PROGRAM
FOR SCHOOL LEADERS
Storyteller: Ernie

A few years ago, I was invited to design and run a leadership development program for a select group of school leaders. I assumed that these individuals had heard enough from leadership gurus and given enough leadership lectures themselves that there wasn't much they didn't already know, or thought they knew, on the topic. I thought that we would make it a better development event if we created an environment that would allow them to build on what they knew, exchange lessons, and challenge one another.

So I decided to set one condition for accepting the invitation: There would not be any lectures on leadership, by me or by anyone else.

The Preparation

Unfamiliar Environments

Ownership of the Learning

Learning Exchange
Balancing Task and Learning
Linking
Holistic Involvement of the Individual

The sponsoring organization agreed to my one condition and sent a note to all the participants, reiterating that this would be different from any leadership development program they had previously experienced. The focus would be on leadership in general and school leadership in particular. Each participant was asked to bring a laptop and one or two questions related to very real and current leadership challenges that he or she was willing to present to the other participants for help in analyzing and resolving.

In the letter, we reminded them of the primary goals of the program: to learn from one another about leadership and learning; to walk away with answers to or challenging questions about the dilemmas each person brought; to link the overall workshop experience to leading and learning back on the job; to make some friends whom they could contact for support beyond the workshop; and to try out some new concepts, behaviors, and practical tools.

The Launch

The workshop began informally on a Sunday evening over dinner, giving us some time to meet socially.

Holistic Involvement of the Individual

Then, on Monday morning, we all gathered in a very comfortable conference room. I had taped five flip-chart pages to the wall and labeled each with a different day of the week. I placed our chairs in a circle and removed all the tables except one, which was used for water and supplies—markers, tape, and Post-it notes.

I reminded them of the broad outcomes and gave them a brief overview of the week. When I pointed to the five blank flip-chart pages and said with a smile, "There's our design," I detected a little bit of apprehension. I hastened to add that we would fill those pages with our agenda within the next three hours.

I contracted my Learning Coach role as fulfilling the following responsibilities: (1) assisting them in putting together a design for the week; (2) helping them to create some operational norms that would allow us to achieve our outcomes; (3) introducing concepts and tools just in time as needs and opportunities arose; (4) serving as a resource person along the way when appropriate and required; and (5) providing one-on-one coaching as desired. They accepted my offer.

Learning Coach
Safe Environment
Just-in-Time Intervention
One-on-One Coaching Support

We began by identifying a few questions that everyone agreed would be good topics for introductions. For example, "Where have you lived internationally?" "Why did you select this profession?" "What is some accomplishment that gives you a sense of pride and satisfaction?" This not only served to start building the network but also provided an opportunity to establish connections among us at a more integral level. I then explained the process we would be using.

Guided Reflection

Each person wrote one challenge stated as a question on a small Post-it. Next, we heard the challenge questions that each participant wanted to explore along with a bit of background and rationale for the question. We collectively grouped their notes into categories on a flip-chart. After all the questions had been introduced and grouped, participants were invited to put a mark next to the questions they were most interested in addressing.

During a break, two group members took this list of prioritized topics and organized the questions into an agenda, leaving some time on the last afternoon for any questions that might emerge during the week. After the break, the two presented their agenda with the rationale for sequencing, and we quickly agreed that we had a good plan.

Participants decided to work on most questions as a group; however, they agreed to address a few questions simultaneously by breaking into subgroups. Each person volunteered to take the lead for at least one session. In most cases, the leader would be the person who had raised the question or the person with the most passion for the topic.

Just-in-Time Intervention ▷

One-on-One Coaching Support ▷

Ownership of the Learning ▷

I gave the group twenty minutes to allow leaders to prepare for their individual sessions and introduced a planning template they could use if they thought that might be appropriate. I made myself available to the leader of the first session and provided him with support in thinking through his session.

All participants wanted to capture the proceedings of every session and agreed to take turns recording the key outcomes on their laptops.

The Program

We were ready to go. Most of the questions raised in the first session dealt with specific leadership challenges, and as a result everyone was very keen on offering advice and providing support. The extraverts in the group (most were extraverts) couldn't wait to jump in and give their solutions. Some of them took up quite a bit of airtime, and I could see some anxious looks on the faces of those who had something to add but couldn't find a way to wiggle into the monologue. And the introverts in the group were not listening at all as they were still getting their thoughts together. So at an appropriate moment, I stepped in and offered a very simple process that would allow everyone to contribute his or her thoughts.

I handed out Post-its to everyone and suggested that participants write down their ideas or suggestions in the form of headlines or brief phrases so that the recorder and the question owner for the session would have something to remind them of all the input. I also suggested that questions would be perhaps even more valuable than solutions.

I asked them to phrase their questions as "I" questions rather than "you" questions and to focus on some of the underlying issues and assumptions that the question owner could explore before identifying the best solution. This technique—Stop, Reflect, Write, Report—introduces subtleties in asking questions. Many times we ask questions that are leading and judgmental, and this technique encourages a different type of inquiry. They tried this technique and discovered that the extraverts did some good editing, the introverts were able to think using their preferred way, and when they were ready to share what they had written, everyone was listening.

At the end of the exchange, the other participants passed their Post-its to the person who was capturing the ideas and questions, and these were entered into the session summary that was later shared with the whole group. They found this process extremely valuable as it equalized participation, and proceeded to use it throughout the workshop.

At the end of the day, after the exchange, I suggested we have a reflection and dialogue session so that group members could extract the nuggets of learning from the day and link insights from the various sessions. I offered to run the first of these sessions but noted that I would assign subsequent sessions to others. The purpose of doing this was to transfer ownership and give group members opportunities to try out immediately what they were learning, getting individual support from me as a coach.

On Thursday morning, we identified and worked on a few new questions. In order to present the participants with another

Just-in-Time Intervention

Learning and Personality Styles

Guided Reflection

Unfamiliar Environments ▷

Feedback Learning Exchange ▷

Linking ▷

Five Dimensions System ▷

Ownership of the Learning ▷

Guided Reflection ▷

unfamiliar learning environment, we organized a round of team golf, although several were not golfers at all.

We intentionally spread out the beginners and the experts among three teams in order to encourage teamwork and experiential learning. This arrangement especially gave some the opportunity to experience what students may feel—the "not knowing" feeling. Afterward, we had a debrief during which the group analyzed how the unusual setting allowed them to extract lessons about teaming and the discomfort of learning and how that connected to their roles as leaders and teachers.

The Success Factors

On Friday we completed work on the outstanding challenges and then had a thorough session in which we debriefed not only what we had accomplished but how we had accomplished it. We identified the implications and opportunities for leading and learning back on the job.

Participants all felt that this had been the most effective leadership development program they had experienced. And when they listed the reasons why, they unintentionally identified most of the principles and elements of ARL.

- The outcomes were systemic. The participants were able to see the interconnectedness of the personal attitudes, the skills and competencies, the organizational contexts, the specifics of the challenges, and the teams.

- The design was organic. It was tailored to their needs, challenges, and interests, which made it relevant to them. They owned the agenda, and their challenge questions were the primary focus of the workshop.

- They especially valued their colleagues' input to their challenges being given in the form of questions.

- They realized that their tacit knowledge was much more extensive than they had imagined.

- Their mental models about teaching, learning, and leading were challenged.

- The reflection and dialogue sessions helped them extract meaning and link their lessons to their jobs and homes.

- The norms they set for themselves provided a safe environment for learning.

- The learning environment was appreciative and fun and allowed multiple opportunities for learning exchanges.

- For some, the team golf experience had been an unfamiliar setting that triggered new reflections. For all, it provided experiential learning about teamwork and leadership as well as the relationship between teaching and learning.

- As coach, I was able to provide just-in-time insights and practical tools they could try out immediately as well as balance time spent on the task (content) with time spent on the learning (process).

Summary

The multi-day program produced results at many levels. One tangible product was a five-chapter booklet, "Leadership and Learning," that participants wrote, a chapter for each day. They experienced and tried out numerous very simple but practical concepts, tools, and techniques similar to those described in this book, such as Stop, Reflect, Write, Report and reflection and dialogue sessions, that they could try out immediately back home. Many of them changed or refined their thinking on the interrelationships among teaching, learning, teamwork, and leading. All of them now had a group of colleagues and friends to call upon for future "coaching." And I came away convinced that this was a good process for developing educational leaders and learners.

SUMMING UP

In this chapter, we have taken you to different geographic locations and settings, but all had something in common: ARL was being applied in educational settings. Whether the learning happened as a result of an organizational intervention, in a classroom, or in a development program, these stories suggest that when the elements characterizing ARL are included in the design, learning and change happen in amazing ways.

CHAPTER 5

Other Applications
of ARL

At the next two stops on our journey, we take you to some unusual settings. Unusual because when we talk about learning methodologies, the images that typically come to mind are training or teaching situations. Now, as our opening vignette with Jack has shown, learning happens in many different ways and in innumerable, varying contexts; we want to offer two more stories that portray how the ARL elements may be applied.

The first one is a session at a traditional HR conference; the second is a brief session with a sales force looking for a motivational speaker to provide inspiration. Both became learning experiences of great value for the participants, and we believe that the ARL elements that guided the interventions played a major role in the results. Again, we include boxes showing the ARL elements.

CONFERENCES CAN BE DIFFERENT
Storyteller: Isabel

The organizers of a very formal conference of human resources and organizational development professionals invited me to give a presentation about ARL.

A Formal Setting

Upon entering the conference hall the day before my presentation, I was dismayed by the extreme formality of the setting. All presenters lectured from a raised stage to hundreds of professionals sitting in a theater-like configuration in the large conference room. The size of the audience and the physical layout were, for me, a clear constraint on interactive participation between audience and presenter. I felt increasingly uncomfortable, reflecting on the paradox of giving a formal lecture about a methodology based on reflecting on real actions and on personal experiences. I had printouts of my PowerPoint slides ready for the overhead projector but was feeling very uneasy about the situation.

An Informal Discussion

On the morning of my presentation, I decided that I simply couldn't do what I had planned. I shared my concern with a colleague, and we came up with a different design for the session. We would have a live conversation. I spoke to another colleague and asked if she would be willing to come onstage with me. I explained that she would play the part of a friend stopping by to see me in my home; we would have a spontaneous, unrehearsed conversation, and she would ask me what I was doing. After that, she just had to continue the dialogue in an organic way. She agreed, intrigued by the idea.

During the break, I gave instructions to lower the lights on the stage and leave only a spotlight in the center. I asked the planners to remove the podium and replace it with a table and a couple of chairs. I also asked for two glasses of water, a couple of cups of coffee, and a vase with flowers. The organizers seemed a bit puzzled at first but agreed to my requests. When the session began, the audience was surprised to see a dark stage with a spotlight over a table, and me sitting, browsing through papers, in silence.

In the absence of the customary introduction of the speaker, audience members soon realized that something else was going to happen, and their voices fell into intrigued silence. I made no eye contact with the audience and pretended to work on my papers until there was a ring, and I opened an imaginary door.

At the door was my friend, who cheerfully said that she happened to be in the neighborhood and had decided to stop by to say hello. As she saw the table filled with papers, she asked if I were busy, and I explained that I was preparing a presentation for an HR conference. She asked me about the topic of my lecture, and I replied it was about ARL. She continued asking me, in a very spontaneous and casual way, about the topic. We had coffee and chatted, and as I was answering her questions, I was able to explain what I had planned to say about the ARL approach. I used her just-in-time questions to show her a few slides illustrating my points in an informal way. We had half an hour of wonderful conversation, and I was pleased by the audience's rapt attention; they were clearly enjoying the change of pace. When she finally said she was leaving so that I could finish preparing my session, we hugged good-bye, and the audience exploded into enthusiastic applause.

Unfamiliar Environments

Lively Q&A

I took the microphone, thanked audience members for the applause, and asked them to take a minute of silence and to write down a question each about what they had just heard.

Next, I asked them to hand their questions to facilitators who were standing at the end of the rows and suggested that, while I read the questions, audience members should turn to their neighbors and exchange reactions, questions, and thoughts. The room became very noisy. In the meantime, I sorted and grouped the questions with the help of a colleague.

Guided Reflection

Ownership of the Learning

After a few minutes of lively exchange, I announced that I would respond to some of the questions I had received and asked those whose questions I was unable to address to leave their personal business cards so I could e-mail my replies.

Learning Exchange

In the remaining time, I also answered a few follow-up questions that emerged spontaneously from the interaction.

Learning and Personality Styles

Summary

This was one of the most enjoyable presentation experiences I have had at a conference. The action of the audience in preparing their written questions not only created some ownership among them for the exchange of information but also increased the connection between audience and presenter. I was able to link the experience itself with the methodology I was trying to describe—it became just-in-time learning. Audience members experienced the power of reflection and of exchanging thoughts with their colleagues and witnessed the effectiveness of a few structured slides combined with an organic conversation. I had integrated different learning styles into my presentation. Finally, the atmosphere was lively and appreciative. This encouraged participation; they took risks and asked questions, which was something that had not yet happened during that conference.

CHANGE STARTS WITH ONE SESSION

Storyteller: Isabel

The setting for this story is the Middle East. We were contacted by the leader of a multinational corporation who was organizing a convention and was looking for "some motivational speakers" to inspire and boost the energy of the audience. He described the group of two hundred as in need of more focus so that they could tap into their resources and maximize market opportunities. In addition, he thought that a lack of ownership was manifested in low commitment.

We explained that a one-time session was not the magic bullet for changing morale and that, from a systemic perspective, he and his leadership team had to role-model new behaviors. He agreed, and we arranged to support him in that endeavor.

Still, we offered to run a two-hour session during the convention event, making clear that our approach was not the typical

Sequenced Learning

keynote presentation, as we designed highly participative sessions that promote involvement, reflection, and action.

The Design

After analyzing the context and expectations, we prepared a session called "The Power of a Dream: An Inspirational Session." It began with the ballroom in the dark. We projected a slide show on a large screen and took turns sharing brief stories about individuals who had followed and achieved their dreams.

Unfamiliar Environments

Stories of Dreams

Only our voices were heard in the darkness, creating a very unusual atmosphere; the audience was extremely curious and intrigued. We had selected the stories to portray a variety of achievements, from heroic successes to simple, daily dreams come true that nonetheless made an impact. To capture the attention of the whole audience, we told the stories following Bernice McCarthy's "4Mat" structure covering "what," "why," "how," and "so what."[8] For example, we said, "This is the story of Amanda, a journalist in the Philippines," and gave a few headlines about her special achievement. Then we briefly stated why we had selected this story and how Amanda had made her success happen. We concluded each vignette with a "so what" comment, that is, with reflections on what we could learn and apply from this story.

Learning and Personality Styles

Following the stories we lit the room brightly and addressed the audience, an important step, as we wanted to begin developing trust, and dark rooms tend to create tension. We established visual contact with the participants and began a small debrief of the stories, pointing to the implications and explaining how the achievements of those individuals could be connected with participants' own lives and with our lives.

Safe Environment

Linking

Visualizing Success

Then we introduced the next segment, a visualization exercise. With calming music in the background, we invited audience members to close their eyes and travel in their minds to a quiet place where they could really feel relaxed and connect with themselves. From that place, we asked them to go back mentally to one very satisfying moment of their lives, when they felt proud of themselves and happy with an achievement. We asked them to feel that deep happiness and the level of energy that filled them.

Holistic Involvement of the Individual

We asked them to think of the personal resources and talents that had helped them reach that successful moment. With this image as a background, we invited them to reflect on one current situation in their work environment that made them feel unhappy and in which they could use their personal talents and resources to generate a change.

Guided Reflection Appreciative Approach

The next step was for audience members to imagine that it was a year from now and they were receiving an award for their achievement. We asked participants to think of an acceptance speech mentioning what happened, who helped them, what obstacles they faced, and the impact they made. We had them write some keywords or thoughts on a prepared template. In the belief that dreams that are shared become stronger, we allocated some time for people to share their speeches at their tables.

Coaching and Reflection

One-on-One Coaching Support Just-in-Time Intervention

After the writing session, we asked each participant to engage in a brief coaching conversation with his or her neighbor, for which we provided some quick guidance. The purpose was to explore assumptions about their possible solutions, assess the resources available, identify some concrete next steps, and agree on checking in with this new "partner" on a fixed date so that each could support the other on their dream journeys. As we got closer to the end of the session, we heard a few of the speeches that had been written earlier and invited audience members to reflect on the lessons from this session and exchange them with their partners.

Learning Exchange

Learning and Personality Styles Balancing Task and Learning

Finally, we did a quick summary of what we had done together and why. At that time, the leader announced that a new award had just been created to recognize special achievements. Next year, audience members would have a chance to present the dreams that actually came true.

Sequenced Learning

Summary

This was a unique experience, in which learning happened unexpectedly for audience members. They didn't expect to be learning anything—they were, like Jack in our opening vignette, just going through the day. However, they ended up participating in an event with an enormous impact, which boosted energy more than anticipated and created a heightened level of ownership. Dreams are powerful—but so are designs that pay attention to the ARL elements.

Ownership of the Learning

SUMMING UP

This chapter opened some further avenues for understanding how, when, and in what contexts ARL elements may be applied. Whether it's a conference or a motivational session, what counts is the purpose, the ultimate goal. When the aim is to generate learning, to drive change in behaviors, and to challenge the usual perspectives, mind-sets, or assumptions, the key elements create learning environments that optimize results.

We saw it in these stories. Next, we will hear about it, as Learning Coaches in action tell us how they go about making it happen.

PART THREE

The Learning Coach in Action

In this section, we share new stories with you, but this time you will be hearing the voice of the Learning Coach. You will be able to learn firsthand how this specialized facilitator of learning goes about exploring the needs, designing and planning the interventions, and acting while wearing the various hats of a Learning Coach.

In the following chapters we continue to highlight "just in time" the ARL elements as they appear in the story. You are encouraged to identify for yourself the rationale for each element's inclusion.

CHAPTER 6

One-on-One Coaching

The next stop on the journey is Miami. In the leisurely setting of a South Beach coffee shop, Eric, a Learning Coach, explains to Amy, a new acquaintance, how he has used ARL in individual coaching. While the content and specific focus of any coaching assignment may vary from client to client, the ARL elements provide a sound foundation and checklist.

Let's join their conversation.

TEACHING CLIENTS TO FISH

AMY: So, Eric, what brings you to South Beach?

ERIC: I just finished a coaching session in the neighborhood and thought I would stop by for a coffee.

AMY: Coaching session? Are you getting coached, or do you coach?

ERIC: I'm a coach, a Learning Coach—or more precisely, an Action Reflection Learning coach.

AMY: What's that?

ERIC: I help people learn—about themselves, their work, their teams, their organizations, their careers, how to solve problems, how to make their dreams come true, how to speak up, how to make a difference—all kinds of things.

AMY: How is that different from what a regular coach does?

ERIC: A regular coach is basically concerned with improving performance. As an ARL coach, besides improving performance, I help individuals solve their problems and challenges. At the same time, I help them learn about coaching itself—understanding the processes, concepts, and tools that I use. I do this so that they can use these tools both for themselves and for others without my having to be there. Using a fishing metaphor, my job is to help my clients not only catch fish but also learn about fishing, both at the same time.

Balancing Task and Learning ▷

AMY: So who do you coach?

ERIC: Mostly I coach executives who are interested in becoming more effective managers and leaders or who have specific challenges to face.

AMY: And what is it exactly that you do with them? I've never understood what a coach actually does. If I were an executive and came to you for coaching, what would you say to me?

Ownership of the Learning ▷

ERIC: Well, first, I would ask you why you want a coach. Most of the people I'm coaching have something they want to work on. Sometimes they come of their own volition; sometimes they're sent by their boss or HR for some fine-tuning.

Once I'm aware of the initial reason, I like to clarify my approach to coaching. I might say something like this: "Amy, coaching is an interactive and organic process that will revolve around you—your interests, your challenges, and your questions. I won't answer your questions for you, but I will help you find answers. Along the way, I'll introduce you to practical self-coaching processes and concepts that you can use with yourself and others. I'll ask you open-ended and clarifying questions. I'll challenge your thinking periodically by asking you to examine your assumptions. I assume that ultimately you know what's really best for you, and I'll support you in making that discovery.

You'll have your hands on the steering wheel; I'll be sitting right next to you."

Just-in-Time Intervention

Then I would tell you that in addition to the reason you initially approached me, whatever that was, we can work on a number of related topics during our time together, depending on your interests, needs, and time. For example, you could do any of the following:

- Extract insights from a 360-degree feedback process as well as performance appraisal feedback that would help you prepare your own personal development plan

Feedback

- Map out your career plan

- Identify the legacy you want to leave in your job and in your life and a plan to make them a reality

- Examine your life story and discover patterns, traps, values, drivers, and dreams—all of which could inform your personal development plan

Holistic Involvement of the Individual

- Build your management team into a high-performing team

- Define the life/work balance that you want in your life

- Work on challenges that emerge periodically

Just-in-Time Intervention
Balancing Task and Learning

AMY: Eric, when you say "work on challenges that emerge periodically," are you also referring to business challenges? If so, does an ARL coach simultaneously provide executive coaching and business coaching?

ERIC: Most client challenges that we face as ARL coaches usually fall into two categories—personal relationship and organizational. However, these challenges have a direct impact on the business, so, in an indirect way, the interventions of an ARL coach will have an impact on the business. Since we are not experts in most of the product and service areas of our clients, they are not expecting us to coach them on business-specific matters. And even if we were, we would decline the temptation of telling them what to do. We help our clients find options but leave the final decisions to them.

DEFINING WHAT'S NEEDED

AMY: Eric, I am very curious to know more specifically, with more details, how you help them become more effective managers and leaders.

Ownership of the Learning

ERIC: Most of my clients have a pretty good sense of what they need to work on when I meet them. In one way or another, they are interested in becoming more effective leaders/managers. I combine "leader" and "manager" because most executives have dual roles: leading (inspiring and modeling) and managing (planning, organizing, coordinating, and controlling). Some of the specific ways that I help them include:

Appreciative Approach

- Identifying what they are currently doing well and should continue to do

- Defining potential "career-limiting behaviors" such as poor listening, talking too much, losing one's temper, jumping to conclusions, fear of public speaking, and so on and then designing plans to address each of them

- Defining what is not working in important business relationships and then finding solutions for mending or improving these relationships

- Defining what they can do to be more effective team leaders and managers and then working with them and their teams on raising performance

Five Dimensions System

- Defining what is not working well in their organization and then supporting them in designing solutions

AMY: Eric, it sounds like you first help your clients define what's needed before going to solutions.

ERIC: That's right. Unless we begin with a good definition of the precise problem, we may be seeking a solution for the wrong thing.

AMY: Do any of your clients ever opt to work on all the offers you give them?

ERIC: Sure, I've had a couple of clients who wanted to work on all areas over the period we were together. Those have been the most enjoyable coaching experiences for me because the approach has been more systemic and integrated. And I believe that the results were more dramatic and easier to sustain as a consequence.

Five Dimensions System

However, I encourage all my clients to begin with a 360-degree feedback survey, which gives them feedback not only from their boss but also from their direct reports and peers. This feedback serves as a rich source for their development plan.

Feedback

And because most of my clients lead teams, many of them want support in developing higher performance in their teams. This is a great opportunity for me to see how they really demonstrate leadership. It's easy for them to talk about how they lead; it's quite another matter, however, to see them shoulder to shoulder with their direct reports. That's where the rubber meets the road.

WHY 360-DEGREE FEEDBACK IS VITAL

AMY: You know, Eric, when you mention that you encourage all your clients to begin with a 360-degree feedback survey, I am inferring that most of your clients have relationship or communication problems with either their peers, boss, direct reports, or other stakeholders. Am I correct? Is 360-degree feedback really a must for all coaching assignments?

ERIC: Well, most of my clients, in fact almost everyone I know, including myself, are working on any number of relationships. And improving these relationships often requires changes from both parties. Communication of one kind or another (contracting, giving and receiving feedback, having difficult conversations, making clear offers and requests, and so on) is always a part of the change process. Most of us have the "gift" of ignoring or burying those sides of ourselves we don't want to look at, and consequently we don't always see ourselves as others do. While 360-degree feedback is not a must, I strongly encourage individuals to go through the process so that they get a more accurate perception of themselves. I'm a strong advocate of a change process that begins within.

AMY: Can you give me an example of how you work with someone on his 360-degree feedback?

ERIC: Sure. When a company has its own 360-degree feedback instrument, I use that; if it doesn't, I will customize to fit the situation. Once my client and I have the summary report, we both take some time to go through it and note the strengths and weaknesses. Then we have a conversation. I get to hear the conclusions and inferences he is making based on the data. I listen at first and summarize periodically what I've heard. Then I ask questions like these:

Guided Reflection ▷

- Why do you think your peers all tended to rate you in a similar way?

- What do you think was running through your boss's mind when she rated you on that point?

Feedback ▷

- Why do you think your boss rated you higher on that item than your direct reports did?

- Why did you rate yourself so low on that item?

- What patterns do you see coming out of this summary?

- How is this similar to or different from other 360-degree feedback you've received before?

My last question would be:

Ownership of the Learning ▷

- What meaning do you take from the overall assessment?

Once we've had a good conversation on the strengths and weaknesses revealed by the 360-degree feedback process, we turn our attention to the "so what" questions:

- So what do you want to keep or increase?

- So what do you want to decrease or let go?

- So what will you do in order to make those changes?

- So what support will you need?

- So what will you say to the folks who have taken their time to give you this feedback?

Learning and Personality Styles Linking

AMY: That sounds like a thorough process! Are there any subtle techniques you use to make this exercise more effective?

ERIC: Yes, there are several. I spend some time with my clients before even deciding to go into a 360-degree feedback process and try to help them accept the notion that feedback is beneficial.

Appreciative Approach

I help them identify times in the past when they received feedback that was extremely helpful. I've found that by creating this appreciative mind-set, my clients are much more open and eager to read the data. Later, when we get to the next steps, I move them from "I want" to "I will." I encourage them to write down their next steps and put concrete time commitments to their "I will" statements. I've found that these simple nuances promote change. The challenge is change.

HELPING CLIENTS CHANGE IN SIGNIFICANT WAYS

AMY: It seems that you spend more time asking questions than providing input, sharing your experience and knowledge.

ERIC: You're right, Amy. As ARL coaches, we believe that questions are the catalysts for learning. A question is a much more powerful tool for finding a solution that really works than a suggestion from me. Answers my clients discover for themselves are much more powerful than recommendations I give because the answers are theirs, not mine. Ownership is a precursor for change.

Ownership of the Learning

AMY: I was just thinking, you're really in the "change business," aren't you? Have you discovered what makes change last?

ERIC: Well, lasting change is almost a paradox, isn't it? But I do believe that it is possible for individuals who want to change to actually make change stick—at least until something better comes along or they are required to change yet again. As human beings, we've made many changes in the process of becoming adults. Some were conscious choices, and other changes happened unconsciously. In the realm of conscious change, there are some basic principles that seem to make a difference. You know, Amy, I just happen to have a presentation that I've prepared on this topic for a conference. So if you're interested, I'll show you some ingredients that support lasting change.

AMY: Sure! Show me!

ERIC: Let me simply walk you through this presentation:

1. **Changing a habit takes time and repetition.** Just to give you a very mundane example, men have a hard time trying to change the direction in which we put on our belt each morning. The same goes for habits of mind. As Mark Twain once said, "Old habits can't be thrown out the upstairs window. They have to be coaxed down the stairs one step at a time." Of course, some habits require less time than others. I set a minimum of six months for most coaching assignments, with a face-to-face or phone meeting every month. It's difficult to learn how to play the piano with only one lesson and no practice between lessons.

   Sequenced Learning ▷

2. **Change requires motivation.** I had a client who made his way through school without really mastering reading, until he was a teenager and received a letter from a girl he liked. His motivation to learn to read was that love letter.

   Ownership of the Learning ▷

3. **Change requires some kind of plan.**[9] Good intentions are not enough. The more complex the change, the more elaborate the plan must be. Define what it is you really want. Then set some targets, strategies, standards, measures, and resources.

4. **Change requires action.** Sometimes we are frozen because of the pressure to be perfect. I suggest that my clients take the "try it out" approach, which is much more freeing than the "getting it perfect" approach. Don't try to run before you can walk.

5. **Change requires support.** A friend, learning partner, support group, and/or coach is vital to sustaining the energy required for serious change.

One-on-One
Coaching
Support

6. **Change requires feedback.** We need some kind of mirror. Asking for feedback is one of the best ways to get it. Feedback is both appreciative and constructive, and I encourage my clients to seek both.

Feedback

7. **Change deserves a reward.** Take time for an appropriate celebration. Looking forward to a reward is also motivating.

8. **Finally, lasting change requires regular reflection.** We need to stop and ask ourselves what we are learning so that we can continually improve and grow. Sharing these lessons with a friend, learning partner, support group, and/or coach reinforces the lessons.

Learning
Exchange

AMY: Wow! I need to ponder all that. Could you send me a copy of your presentation? It would be a helpful reminder to me in my own work. How do you know when change is successful? How do you know when you've made a real difference?

ERIC: Another good question. Generally, my clients know when they have been successful. They can see or feel the difference. It usually begins within and gradually makes itself visible so that their families and friends and colleagues notice that something is different. It depends, of course, on the kind of change a person wants. When it's behavioral, it's easier to measure; when it's attitudinal, it's subtler. However, even attitudinal change leads to behavior change. So I ask my clients, "How will you know when you've successfully changed?" I encourage them at the beginning of the journey to define what success looks like. Usually they have

Ownership of
the Learning ▷

a pretty good idea what to look for, and it helps keep them focused and motivated.

WHAT COULD GO WRONG

AMY: No doubt some of your clients never managed to change. So tell me, what are the ingredients for a failed coaching experience?

ERIC: Give me a moment to collect my thoughts. That's a good question. Let me jot down my thoughts.

AMY: No problem. While you're thinking, I'll get us another cup of coffee.

ERIC [later]: OK, I made a brief list on my napkin. Here are a few ingredients for failure based on my personal experiences as well as the experiences of colleagues:

Sequenced
Learning ▷

- **Not a regular rhythm.** For example, with one client I did not set clear expectations regarding frequency of meetings at the beginning of our relationship, and eventually the times between our sessions grew longer and longer until one day we agreed to end the relationship. It simply wasn't adding value because it was impossible to maintain the momentum and to follow up on the topics of our sessions.

- **Twisted arm.** One client felt forced to enter into a coaching relationship with me. I could feel his reluctance to really engage, and so I suggested that we end the relationship. As soon as he realized that he had some control, he agreed to continue; when it became his decision to continue, it worked.

Ownership of
the Learning ▷

- **Breach of confidence.** One of my colleagues lost a client when he shared a story about the client with another person in the company. He thought he had "adjusted" the story enough so that his client was protected. He hadn't, and the story eventually got back to his client and resulted in a loss of trust and the loss of a client.

Safe Environment

AMY: So why did you become a coach?

ERIC: There's nothing more satisfying than seeing someone make a breakthrough in his or her life. And since I'm working with people who have direct and indirect influence over hundreds of lives, I can see the ripple effect throughout an organization when an executive's attitude and behavior shift for the better. It's very rewarding to know that my small interventions can make a big difference.

Holistic Involvement of the Individual

I was coaching a senior executive at a major multinational corporation, and he showed such a high level of commitment to his learning that he started a learning log to keep track of his reflections. He was eager and curious, asked lots of questions, and at each session shared with me how he was trying to apply the coaching techniques with his own subordinates. I can't tell you how satisfying that was to witness.

AMY: Eric, as I listen to you, I have more and more questions! Did you say you also coach teams? What do you do with them? And what knowledge or experience does a coach need? Are there specific skills or characteristics? So many questions, and I'm running out of time, Will you be around tomorrow?

ERIC: By all means, let's get together again. I've enjoyed our conversation; this has been a great reflective activity for me. What about meeting here tomorrow, at the same time?

SUMMING UP

This conversation portrays the application of ARL to individual coaching. One-on-one coaching doesn't have to be business related; it can be applied to any type of individual coaching—with a peer, a friend, or a family member. And when a coach applies the

ARL methodology, the coaching experience becomes a powerful learning intervention. When individuals are coached based on the ARL approach, they actually learn about themselves and about human interactions. The coach becomes the facilitator for that learning. While many coaches spontaneously include a number of the elements, ARL-based coaching pays attention to all of them.

Eric and Amy will meet again to follow up on their conversation. This time, they will explore how ARL was applied with a dysfunctional team.

CHAPTER 7

A Team Turnaround

In this chapter, you will be invited to listen in on the second conversation between the ARL coach, Eric, and his friend Amy. This time, he will describe the challenges of an underperforming team with low morale and the interventions that helped turn the team around.

Let's rejoin Eric and Amy now.

AMY: Good morning, Eric. Thanks again for that stimulating conversation yesterday. Now I'm eager to hear how ARL coaching can help teams and teamwork—especially teams in trouble. There are a couple of teams in my organization that need to make a real turnaround, and I'm leading one of them.

ERIC: Amy, I enjoyed our conversation yesterday as well. I thought I could share with you the story of a team that made, as you put it, a "real turnaround." As the name implies, Action Reflection Learning is a reflective process, and "reflection" applies to the coach's planning of the work as well as to the actual interactions. So I'll start with what happened *before* the team's work started.

THE PLANNING PROCESS

ERIC: A couple of years ago, Craig, a senior leader in the corporate marketing function of a multinational company, approached me in the company cafeteria. Craig told me that his boss, Sonja, the global VP of marketing, was looking for a coach for both herself and her international team. According to Craig, Sonja's leadership team was not functioning very well. He wanted to know if I was interested in working with Sonja.

AMY: What do you mean "not functioning very well"?

ERIC: Craig told me that many of the members of the team, his peers, made excuses and didn't even show up at global marketing meetings, saying that the meetings were a waste of time. Apparently, the meetings were not well planned; many topics were discussed over and over with no resolution; some individuals took too much airtime, while others hardly participated; there wasn't a sense of purpose, and no one knew what the priorities were; the team didn't have a clear sense of direction; Sonja wasn't holding individuals or the team accountable; and the atmosphere wasn't safe, so most team members felt inhibited about speaking up. Craig said that Sonja seemed to avoid tough, confrontational issues. As a consequence, there were a lot of unresolved issues. Some team members were even starting to question Sonja's ability to lead.

AMY: So where do you begin in a case like this?

ERIC: Well, I needed to begin with Sonja. So I asked Craig if Sonja felt there was a problem. He said probably so, as she had confided to him that leading the team was very frustrating. I told Craig that Sonja's acknowledgment was the best place to start, an awareness of how things were. Craig gave her a quick call to let her know that I was willing to work with her. She agreed to see me in half an hour.

AMY: So what happened?

ERIC: Sonja began by saying that she was happy I was willing to work with her, but unfortunately she only had half an hour right then. So I suggested that we both jot down our questions. She had two: Who are you, and how do you work as a coach? My questions to her were: Why do you want a coach, and what are you looking for in a coach?

AMY: Why did you ask her to write down her questions?

ERIC: I've discovered that taking a moment to think improves and deepens the quality of the conversation. Introverts, like me, really appreciate this time to reflect; extraverts, although they prefer to think out loud, benefit from a little "editing" time.

Learning and Personality Styles

AMY: I see . . . What did she say?

ERIC: She admitted that her primary interest in coaching was to get help in turning her team around. She then went on to describe some of the current team behaviors and painted a picture of her team that was very similar to what Craig had portrayed. She said she had inherited the team from her predecessor soon after the merger a year ago, and that since then they had never really gelled as a team and consequently weren't really working together. She told me that they had an off-site meeting coming up in six weeks and thought it might be a time to address some of the problems she had outlined. She then asked me to tell her about myself and my approach to coaching teams.

AMY: Do you mind spelling out what you told her about your approach? I'm very curious.

ERIC: Sure. I told her that in general my goal in coaching is to help individuals and teams create the conditions under which they can speak up freely and say what is on their minds and in their hearts. And that this goal is based on the assumption that everyone has a contribution to make and wants to add value regardless of his or her position and role, and all people need is a safe space and a good process that enables them to speak up and be heard. So, in short, my job was to help Sonja and her team create that safe space and find those appropriate processes.

AMY: What do you mean by "safe space"?

ERIC: To me, a safe space is an environment without retribution, where people won't be punished for speaking up. In fact, they are encouraged to speak up, especially if they have an opinion that is entirely different from everybody else's. And a helpful process we use with teams in creating this safe space is to set norms—their ground rules for working together. As I continue the story, you'll see other processes that contribute to creating a safe space and empowering individuals to speak up.

GETTING TEAM FEEDBACK

AMY: Please go on with the story. You were telling Sonja about your approach.

ERIC: That's right. I told Sonja that in our next conversation I would like to know a bit more about the team—who the team members were and what roles they played, their history together, the team's purpose, key stakeholders, Sonja's role, what seemed to be working well and what wasn't working so well, and what she saw as her leadership goals. This would give me two important pieces of information: first, the current status of the team (at least from Sonja's perspective), and second, an opportunity to calibrate her perception with Craig's.

Then I offered to help her with her off-site meeting and suggested some steps to take:

1. Sonja should write a note to her team members, letting them know that she had contracted me to work with her and her team and that I would support them in their off-site meeting. In preparation for the meeting, participants should send me at least one question they wanted addressed during the meeting. I, in turn, would organize their questions into a survey and send it out to them.

They would then send their responses back to me, giving me enough time to prepare a survey summary with all of their comments included verbatim. I would return the summary to them immediately before the off-site meeting as pre-meeting reading.

Ownership of the Learning

2. She would invite a couple of team members to work with me in identifying outcomes in five dimensions—company or business, organization, team, professional, and personal—and then we would co-design the meeting together.

Five Dimensions System

3. She would have input along the way to ensure that her voice was included and she felt comfortable with the direction we were taking.

AMY: That's a lot of pre-meeting work! What are the benefits?

ERIC: Yes, it is a lot of work. But by getting the team members' questions in advance, I'm able to discover what is really important to them. Their questions are a better diagnostic instrument than questions I might ask, although I do add some questions to the survey from time to time. And because the questions are theirs, they are more motivated to answer them. They own the questions as well as the answers. The meeting actually begins several weeks beforehand with the survey. Sometimes I conduct interviews instead if there's adequate time. This allows us to focus pretty quickly on the issues once we all get together face-to-face. Plus it helps me develop rapport with the team.

Ownership of the Learning

AMY: Do you make the survey anonymous?

ERIC: Yes, because sometimes team members clean up their responses if the survey is not anonymous for fear of reprisal or of standing out. Anonymity encourages openness and honesty. Ultimately, I want to create an environment where anonymity is not necessary for team members to speak out. But anonymity usually helps at the beginning.

AMY: How do you create an environment where anonymity is not necessary? How long does it take you as coach to get team members to feel comfortable being open and honest with the boss and among themselves—without requiring anonymity?

ERIC: As I mentioned earlier, setting norms is one strategy. Another is to encourage the team leader to sincerely request honesty and openness and offer a commitment not to "kill the messenger." Sometimes I coach the leader in not only what to say but, more important, how to say it.

Safe Environment

One-on-One Coaching Support

In this case, as you will see, Sonja was able to quickly defuse the fear and create an atmosphere in which her team felt comfortable about speaking up. The leader sets the tone and is key in opening the door to honest dialogue.

AMY: You said the outcomes are defined by several people? How is that?

ERIC: Well, I've come to realize over the years that ideally every team member should have a say in the outcomes; this creates real ownership and begins to build a positive atmosphere.

AMY: So then what do you do with the interview or survey summary other than send it out to the team members?

ERIC: The content of the survey gives us a pretty good idea about the issues we should address during the meeting. So it influences the design process. And the content is used as a reference throughout the meeting as a source of wisdom and as a compass.

AMY: What happened with your offer to support Sonja?

ERIC: She sent out the letter as I suggested and invited two members of her executive team to join me on the design team. The three of us met virtually several times without Sonja. We first identified possible outcomes and then put together a draft design before presenting it to Sonja and getting her buy-in.

Once I got the survey back from her team, I added three very important questions. First, in order for our team to become a higher-performing team, what should Sonja continue to do that she is already doing? Second, what should Sonja consider stopping or doing less? And third, what should Sonja consider starting or

Feedback   doing more?

The feedback was powerful and really gave Sonja a clear sense of what she needed to do. It was also empowering. Her team was encouraging her to make those tough decisions she was avoiding, to hold them accountable, to set clear directions, to run more effective meetings, to invite them to share the leadership so she wouldn't feel that everything was on her shoulders, to take more time to meet with them individually and collectively, and simply to listen to what they were thinking and feeling.

AMY: How did Sonja take this feedback?

ERIC: I was a bit concerned that she might get angry with the feedback and try to figure out who said what or go into denial. However, I was pleasantly surprised when I met with her before the session to offer her some support. She said she felt the feedback was fair and expected. In fact, she said it was a bit of a relief to receive it; her leadership or lack of leadership was no longer a "dead moose" in the middle of the room. However, she was not sure how to address this in public.

One-on-One Coaching Support

We discussed her options and preferences on acknowledging the feedback to her team. We considered this acknowledgment a very important issue for all members of the group who had taken the risk of giving their feedback. They probably would be anxious to see her reactions and read her body language. So we decided that she would talk about it at the very beginning, during the kick-off. The off-site meeting was to be held at this very old, historic, and beautiful hotel in the countryside. We planned an informal opening around the fireplace—a perfect, relaxed setting for launching an honest and open conversation.

THE KICKOFF

ERIC: So there we were, sitting around in a comfortable room with a cozy fireplace at the beautiful hotel. Sonja offered everyone a glass of wine and invited team members to make themselves comfortable. After a big smile and a welcome toast, she thanked them for showing up and making the meeting a priority. She told them she was particularly grateful for their candid feedback on the three questions related to her leadership. She said she valued that feedback as a real sign of interest and support and was going to make some significant changes related to all their suggestions.

Appreciative Approach

She went on to say that in the next few days she would be making specific commitments addressing each of their suggestions. She added that she needed their help and would make specific requests of them in turn. She ended by saying that the success of their team was in their collective hands.

The ice was broken; the first climate for a productive meeting session had been established. The unspoken concerns about Sonja's leadership—the "dead moose" as Sonja had put it earlier—had begun to be addressed.

AMY: What a wonderful beginning! So far you've mentioned only Sonja's difficulties. What about the problems and conflicts among the team members themselves? Did they exist? Were they surfaced and tackled?

ERIC: Yes, there were a number of interpersonal issues within the team as well. As in every team, some individuals didn't get on as well with some members as they did with others. As an example, one team member was brutally honest with her feedback, which came across more like criticism. She had offended almost everyone at some point during her tenure on the team. One of the team norms that everyone agreed to was providing timely feedback in a

Safe Environment

caring manner.

During the meeting, this individual received caring feedback from a couple of her peers when her critical comments landed like hand grenades. And surprisingly, she responded well and tempered her comments throughout the meeting. There were other examples as well. However, Sonja's leadership challenge was key to unlocking some of the other interpersonal issues.

AMY: How did Sonja engage the team in helping her?

ERIC: Going into the meeting, people were very anxious, since they all had read the feedback Sonja received. So once she addressed it right up front, there was a great sense of relief. The next morning, we took some time to exchange perspectives on the survey in the form of a dialogue.

AMY: You discussed it?

ERIC: Well, what I mean by dialogue is actually a type of conversation that is unlike most discussions, which have frequent interruptions and generally poor listening going on. I created a safe environment for speaking up and out by setting some ground rules for this particular kind of conversation—for example, to not judge one another and no "ping-ponging" to allow a pause between one comment and the next.

Safe Environment

These ground rules were especially helpful in allowing individuals who were hesitant about speaking in public to make their voices heard. The first ground rule was that we would begin with a few minutes for reflection, when they could all write down their thoughts. A reflection period offers introverts an opportunity to catch their mental breath, which puts them on an equal footing in the conversation. And extraverts benefit by doing some good editing of their thoughts during the reflection period. This obviously fosters better listening as well.

Guided Reflection

The slowing down also promotes equal participation among teams with cultural differences in addition to personal style differences. For example, there were a number of Swedes on the team. They, in general, are more introverted or humble or respectful of others and don't always jump into a conversation right away. So in a team of Americans or Brits, they are quite easily left out of a conversation. The ground rules for dialogue really equalize speaking opportunities for everyone.

Learning Exchange

AMY: I like this concept of using dialogue. I think we could use it, too, even if it's not related to a survey.

ERIC: Certainly! I've used dialogue sessions to improve the quality of group discussions on almost any topic. Dialogue is not meant to substitute for good debate. However, because it encourages everyone to speak up, debate is often limited and decision making comes easier. It's almost a paradox: When a group doesn't have the pressure of making decisions, group members are more relaxed and listen better; as a consequence, they develop an appreciation for other perspectives, which in turn makes it easier for them to make better decisions.

Dialogue sessions have even been used as a "time out" kind of technique for negotiations of all kinds. If you're interested in learning more, there are many articles and books about dialogue in a variety of applications.

Just-in-Time Intervention

AMY: Really!? Yes, I would like to learn more about it.

ERIC: OK then, find *On Dialogue* by David Bohm, or look up David Isaacs, who worked with Peter Senge. He's done a lot of work using dialogue.

Balancing Task and Learning

After the dialogue, I gave team members a chance to identify questions we needed to address during the meeting that weren't already on the agenda. I intentionally kept a time slot open for addressing these questions.

Guided Reflection

THE SECOND DAY

AMY: So what happened next?

ERIC: To help Sonja deliver on her promises, we began the morning of the second day with the norm-setting session. Sonja and her team identified norms that would lead to higher team performance. These became the ground rules that everyone agreed to live by both during team meetings and between meetings. We converted these norms into the "High-Performing Team Instrument." And during the final session, team members used this instrument to give themselves feedback on how they had performed.

Then, later in the meeting, we had a team–leader contracting session. This was an opportunity for Sonja to write down her "offer" to the team (a list of behaviors the team could expect from Sonja) and her "request" (a list of behaviors she needed and wanted from the team). At the same time, the team was writing down its offer and request for Sonja. When everyone was ready, the team and Sonja exchanged and discussed their respective requests and offers, making slight changes, until both parties agreed on what to accept. This process was very empowering for both Sonja and her team. We put together a written summary of the items on which they agreed, and called it the "Team–Leader Contract." This was an effective way of expressing and agreeing on mutual expectations—which happens to be a way to give feedback to each other—and it heightened the levels of ownership.

AMY: How did the team follow up on all these things?

ERIC: Well, I encouraged all participants to have edited copies of the "Team–Leader Contract" and the "High-Performing Team Instrument" at hand so that they could review these both periodically, see how they were doing as a team, and agree on any changes they needed to make.

AMY: What did you do with all the questions you collected at the start?

ERIC: Oh, yes, we did an Open Space . . .

AMY: What's "Open Space"?

ERIC: "Open Space" is a label a fellow named Harrison Owen gave to a very old idea—the break. Coffee break, tea break, or, as the Swedes call it, *Fika*. During a break, people connect with one another around questions that are on their minds at that given moment. The ground rules of Open Space are pretty simple: first, the people who show up are the right people; second, when it's over, it's over; third, you come and go without it becoming a big deal— simply use your two feet and move on; fourth, you can actively participate or just listen in. These ground rules can be adapted while keeping the spirit of a break, which is informal and pretty relaxed. Often the most productive work takes place in this kind of atmosphere.

Sequenced Learning

**Guided
Reflection**

**Ownership of
the Learning**

**Just-in-Time
Intervention**

AMY: Did you do a breaklike session?

ERIC: Well, I had asked them to write down the questions they wanted to address. So later I invited people to read out their questions, and we quickly grouped them on a flip-chart and designated a cluster leader. That person was responsible for leading a conversation or planning session around a topic and any related questions. Those who were interested followed that person to a different room or corner of the room.

To help them work on their topics, I offered a planning template. Individuals were allowed to stay and work on one question or move from subgroup to subgroup, contributing where they had interest. At the end of the session, everyone got back together, and the group leaders reported on what had happened. In some cases they made group decisions, or at a minimum they agreed on clear next steps. So progress was made in addressing important questions.

AMY: It sounds like fun.

ERIC: It usually is, because people have a chance to influence and decide on the agenda and where they want to go as well as the level of effort and energy they want to invest. Leadership is shared; individuals take responsibility. Very seldom do individuals disappear.

AMY: And how did they do as a team over the course of the event?

ERIC: Pretty well. Of course, a few of them reverted to some old, familiar behaviors from time to time, but now they had an agreed-upon standard and the license to provide just-in-time feedback to one another. And Sonja had established a powerful role model the first evening by welcoming feedback. So this helped as well. Along the way, I reinforced good behavior by noting in my journal when someone tried something out and then letting them know at an appropriate moment that I had noticed.

**Appreciative
Approach**

AMY: Can you give me an idea of some of the other ways you helped the team work?

ERIC: Sure. I basically helped them identify the questions they felt they needed to work on throughout the meeting and suggested appropriate processes to use. At the end of each session, everyone came together as a large group to review the work of the subgroups and report on the progress. And at the end of most sessions, we took some time to debrief not only what we had done but how we had done it. I wanted them to understand the subtleties of the various processes they had just experienced so that they could repeat the processes when I wasn't around. We also identified other areas where they could apply those concepts.

Just-in-Time Intervention

Learning Exchange

Linking

AMY: So I see you're paying attention to the process. I'm curious about what other roles you played.

ERIC: As much as possible, the design team assigned the leadership of different sessions to various members of the team, including themselves. And there were a few sessions that I facilitated. I actually wore a number of hats:

1. I was in charge of the integrity of the design. Although the design team shared in the work, I was the one leading those design sessions—from defining the needs, to agreeing upon the outcomes, to selecting the appropriate design that addressed those outcomes.

2. I was also ensuring that we had a safe environment where our norms were followed. This was everyone's task, but the team relied on me to make sure this happened.

3. I was also available to Sonja and the team members to provide feedback or brief coaching.

4. I had also contracted the role of just-in-time teacher. If I thought there was a concept or tool or technique that would improve the effectiveness and efficiency of the team, I stepped in to make a just-in-time offer.

I was also looking for incidental learning that occurred along the way—especially during breaks and evenings. I would periodically ask after a break or in the morning if someone had an insight or private conversation that might be worth sharing with the entire group; these tended to be very rich exchanges. So I really had my hands full even though I wasn't always facilitating or leading up front.

AMY: That's a lot of hats to wear. Were they aware of what you were doing?

ERIC: Yes. I contracted my role in the very first session so that it wasn't a mystery or a surprise to them. And I needed their OK if I were to truly be empowered to do everything I just mentioned.

AMY: Was there anything you did that made a big difference?

ERIC: Throughout the event, I introduced several other concepts or tools that made the meeting more efficient. In fact, by the end of the meeting, we counted about twenty-four concepts, tools, or techniques we had tried out. However, there was one simple idea that had a big impact.

I had read in the survey summary that many team members felt Sonja was not very good at acknowledging the hard work many of them were doing. So I asked Sonja if she felt this were true, and if so, was she interested in doing something differently. She agreed that giving compliments was a bit difficult for her to do, as she felt people were paid well for doing a good job and shouldn't need her thanks.

I reminded her that many people were motivated by more than money and that a "Thank you" or "Good job!" was extremely motivating and inspired continued high performance—especially if the acknowledgment came from her and was sincere. She agreed, admitting that she, too, appreciated some recognition now and again from her boss.

I suggested that she initiate a toasting ceremony, during dinner, stating that it was time for her and the entire team to recognize the various accomplishments and contributions every team member brought to the team, for individual contributions made the entire team stronger. Sonja was to begin, and the person she toasted would in turn toast someone else until everyone had been toasted.

AMY: So what happened?

ERIC: We had a private room, and Sonja did a super job. She admitted that this was difficult for her, but she realized how important it was to recognize the many contributions that everyone on the team was making for the good of the team and the entire organization. Her toast set a wonderful standard, and everyone could tell that Sonja really meant what she said. The evening ended on a real high, with laughter and some tears along the way. One team member said at the end of the toasts, "Team, after yesterday, today, and this evening, we've reached a new level of teamwork. We can't go back!"

That dinner activity was another turning point in the meeting as well as in their life as a team. They came to understand the power of appreciation.

Holistic Involvement of the Individual

Appreciative Approach

AMY: So, besides generating some good feelings, what was the net result of the meeting?

ERIC: Throughout the meeting, Sonja's personal assistant was recording every decision and every next step, which stated who was to do what by when. She also captured the outcomes from each session. Then immediately after the meeting, she and the design team put together a team charter, a forty-four-page booklet that included a list of all the decisions, team norms, the "High-Performing Team Instrument," the "Team–Leader Contract," the outcomes of every session, a meeting schedule, the meeting protocols, plus all the tools and techniques I had introduced. This served as tangible proof of the team's productivity and a benchmark for future meetings.

But probably even more important was the beginning of a shift in attitudes and new behavior from almost everyone—especially from Sonja. They had great appreciation for one another and confidence in themselves as individuals and as a team. They were learning by doing and taking time to slow down and reflect on what they did so that there was a growing consciousness and appreciation of the progress they were making. They were becoming a learning organization.

Balancing Task and Learning

AMY: Tell me, Eric, what happened in future meetings?

ERIC: I joined them in three other off-site meetings and continued in my role as team coach. However, in each subsequent meeting, I purposely played less and less of an active role, encouraging them to share the leadership and facilitation. Most of my work involved coaching individual team members on the side. We've found that it usually takes two to four meetings spread over twelve to eighteen months for a team to go from conscious behavior change to unconscious mastery.

Sequenced Learning

AMY: So how is what you do any different from what a trained facilitator might do?

ERIC: Good question! As I coach an individual or a team, I am conscious of the ARL elements and use them as a guide in both the design and delivery phases of my work. So there's a conscious emphasis on making this a learning experience for my clients as well as helping them to solve whatever individual or team challenges they want and need to address. I am transparent in the "what," "why," "how," and "so what" of my work so that they are able to replicate the process and go beyond what I've done. I'm really building capabilities. And in this process, I always come away with some new insights myself, for I'm constantly learning from and with my clients. That's why I'm called a Learning Coach; I help others learn and, I hope, I'm learning as well.

AMY: And one final question before I have to run, Eric. What was the most difficult moment for you during this assignment?

ERIC: Wow! Let me do some quick reflection. There were many difficult moments, and at times I felt I was riding a roller coaster. OK. The first one that comes to mind is my session with Sonja prior to the meeting. I was a bit nervous that she was going to be defensive and perhaps even angry with me for opening up a can of worms by including the three questions about her. And I knew that if she resisted or got angry with the feedback and wanted to find out who said what, it would be a very hard and long event. I had done a fair amount of planning as to how to help her accept the tough feedback in case she was defensive. Fortunately, she was smart enough and courageous enough to take the feedback as a gift. By modeling this behavior, she allowed everyone on the team to be open to appreciative and constructive feedback.

AMY: Thanks. You've given me a lot to think about. I'd like to try out a couple of ideas that you've mentioned with one of the teams I'm currently leading. Thank you!

ERIC: You're welcome, Amy. I've come to realize that what I really do is help my clients become conscious of the processes and the conditions that allow them to lead and work as a team. Let me leave you with a quote from one of my favorite books, *The Tao of Leadership,* by John Heider: "Whether you are leading a group or going about your daily life, you need to be conscious. You need to be aware of what is happening and how things happen. Consciousness or awareness, then, is the source of your ability."[10]

SUMMING UP

Helping a team become high performing is a process that begins before the actual team development workshop. It begins with a careful exploration of context, needs, and expectations. It requires detailed layout of the program and attentive design that involves the participants. In this chapter, we described the intricacies of the "getting ready" phase of planning an intervention with a dysfunctional team. Then we showed how Eric applied ARL elements while working with Sonja's team. Along the way, he was not only conscious of helping Sonja and her team catch their fish, a leader who leads and a team that works, but also of teaching them to fish—that is, learning about the processes that enable leaders to lead and high-performing teams to perform at a high level.

In this chapter, you saw how a Learning Coach meets the challenges and complex contexts of ARL. Chapter 8 reveals a coach's inner perspective.

Cascading Change in the Organization

Continuing our journey, this chapter relates how the ARL methodology was used to guide a large manufacturing site through a significant change process.

The plant belonged to a multinational corporation and was initially facing an uncertain future, which was negatively affecting the morale, retention, and performance of its staff. We used ARL tools to support the leader and his executive team in crafting a shared vision and strategy that would engage and motivate the entire organization in executing the needed changes. This required shaping a new organizational culture in a change effort designed to cascade leadership and responsibility for executing a change strategy throughout the plant. As change can provide a wonderful environment for learning, the elements of the ARL learning methodology were used to guide the change process and extract lessons along the way. This makes the ARL elements a powerful option to consider for OD interventions.

The story of the process is captured through the journal entries of one of the three Learning Coaches who designed and implemented the process. For each journal entry, we have two sections—one with the account of the significant events and one with reflections, encompassing the coach's thoughts and feelings about what happened. While these thoughts and feelings are re-created, the events occurred as described.

As in the previous chapters, you are now familiar enough with the ARL elements to be able to identify them as they are implemented to enable this transformational change process.

MAY 8: WE HEAR THE CHALLENGE

Today we met with the site manager, Robert, and his HR manager, Ruby, to hear about the need for change at their site. We learned that due to a number of conditions—global competition, over-capacity, pressure on margins, change in manufacturing strategy, and a new VP (just to name a few)— the future of their site and its more than five hundred employees is uncertain at best. To complicate matters, Robert is the fourth site manager in the past six years, and what is seen by many as revolving leadership is beginning to have an impact on the workforce. Rumors are rampant. Talent is leaving. Morale is sinking, although remarkably product quality has not been adversely affected—yet. However, the new global supply chain leader has recently delivered a sobering challenge: "Frankly, the market changes mean you can't depend on head-quarters for long-term employment. It is time to grow up and take responsibility for your own future."

The writing on the wall seems to be clear and chilling. Robert and his direct reports who form the leadership team (LT) have limited time in which to figure out what kind of manufacturing site they want to become, develop a plan, and then transform themselves and lead the transformation of their site.

The LT is mostly new and still in formation, as several key people recently left. Robert himself is only several months into the job. Robert and Ruby are asking for help. They would like to see the organization transform from a passive, demotivated, complaining organization into a proactive, self-confident culture.

Reflections

We are familiar with this industry and know that it is going through some major changes.

Our team had prepared a list of questions in advance of the meeting to help us explore both overt and covert conditions at the plant. Initially, we focused on building positive perceptions of how the site views the current leadership, because we sensed that unless the LT first formulates and then demonstrates a revitalized leadership role, chances of success are remote.

Guided Reflection

We realized that we will need to develop a systemic solution for their complex set of needs. We felt that the whole organization must be involved in the change, and that following new, clear leadership, all levels must be involved in contributing to the effort if change is to be successful.

Five Dimensions System

We have the advantage that Robert understands our process. We have worked with Robert before, and he is very familiar with our ARL approach and processes and knows that they work. While Ruby is new to ARL, she seemed ready to embrace it instinctively when we described our learning philosophy to her.

MAY 12: WE HAVE A PROPOSAL

I can see how important it is that right after our first meeting, we agreed as a team of Learning Coaches to share the leadership among us. We as coaches need to model the kind of teamwork people want to attain. Many times they tell us that they learn more from what they see us doing than from what we say. And shared leadership is one of the messages we want to convey because it increases power, energy, and ownership.

Today we submitted a three-phase change strategy that focuses first on building up the core of change leaders and then cascades responsibility for, and ownership of, execution of the new strategy throughout the next level of management. The strategy follows this model of progressive transfer of tools, know-how, and empowerment. We as Learning Coaches deliberately attempted to remove ourselves from the roles of "leader" and "expert" so as to facilitate the transfer of knowledge to the client body. The goals of the three phases follow.

Phase 1 Goal: Define the Challenge and Assess Strengths

We want to support the LT in coming to grips with the dimensions of the change challenge ahead and what it will take to develop a scenario for achieving a viable future. To do this, we will focus on the strengths of plant personnel and on their successful history of managing past challenges. From this review, we will guide them to craft the dream scenario as a "pull" strategy.

Appreciative Approach

A critical element of the whole effort must be the development of the LT into a high-performing team, which needs to be perceived as a vital leadership force that will formulate a viable plan for the plant's future as well as model the leadership behaviors that will motivate and engage the next level of leadership. The second line of leaders in the organization will be largely responsible for executing the agreed-upon strategy. They are called the next-level leadership team (NLLT). During this phase, we will play an active facilitation and coaching role.

Just-in-Time Intervention

Phase 2 Goal: Build the Leadership Team

In this phase, we want to coach the LT and the NLLT on becoming an integrated leadership team whose members share a future vision, are clear on their strategy, have clearly contracted their distinct roles and responsibilities, and have agreed upon an action plan. A key part of the process is for the integrated leadership team to explicitly capture its learnings in the five dimensions as well as incorporate the ARL tools and processes in its work. These tools will in effect form a new language with which the whole organization will communicate in the future. During this phase, we will share the facilitation task with the LT while providing just-in-time coaching.

Balancing Task and Learning

Just-in-Time Intervention

Phase 3 Goal: Support the New Leaders

In this phase, the goal is to support the new champions (members of the LT and the NLLT) in rolling out the cultural transformation, the strategy, and the learning concepts and tools to the rest of the organization. This process of institutionalizing the learnings and tools will mean that members of the integrated leadership team must coach their direct reports and provide the processes and tools that will enable them to engage the entire workforce in the change to come. During this phase, we will play a shadow coaching role with some preplanned skill-building activities and just-in-time interventions on a limited and as-needed basis. See Figure 2.

FIGURE 2. **Change Strategy Phases 1, 2, and 3**

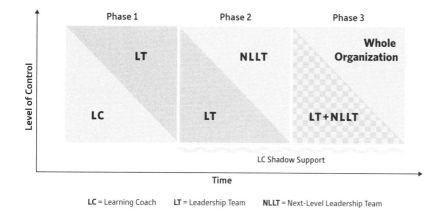

LC = Learning Coach   LT = Leadership Team   NLLT = Next-Level Leadership Team

We explained to Robert and Ruby that our goal with them was threefold:

- Help them create and navigate a successful transformational change

- Make the change process transparent so that they become fluent with the ARL principles, elements, and processes supporting the change

- Encourage them to try out the concepts, tools, and techniques that will make this change endure with their own teams and peers. The team will be responsible for institutionalizing the learnings, behaviors, and new corporate language throughout the manufacturing plant.

Balancing Task and Learning

Ownership of the Learning

Holistic Involvement of the Individual

Just-in-Time Intervention

Guided Reflection

Balancing Task and Learning

Reflections

This is going to be a challenging assignment and will require effective teamwork and modeling on our part.

We are going to need LT input and buy-in for phase 1, the LT is going to need NLLT input and buy-in for phase 2, and the integrated leadership team (the LT and the NLLT) is going to need input and buy-in from the larger site for phase 3.

Throughout the transformational process, we, the consulting team, will need to provide just-in-time concepts, tools, feedback, observations, and questions so that all participants develop an appetite for learning about themselves, leadership, teamwork, change, and organizational effectiveness.

Ownership of the learning, engagement, and power sharing are going to be the levers for this transformational change.

The three of us need to be aware of the overall cascading strategy as we embark on each phase so that we can shift our role accordingly from being more facilitative and visible to serving more as coaching and background support.

We feel we are now mentally and emotionally ready for this challenge.

MAY 15: WE CONTRACT, PLAN, AND ENGAGE

We met with Robert and Ruby to review our three-phase proposal. They accepted our strategy, so we embarked on designing phase 1, which is to turn the LT into a high-performing team that will clarify its mission, define its vision, and learn and then transfer what it has learned to the next level of the organization. With the aim of broadening LT ownership of the program design process, we suggested that Robert and Ruby invite one other member of the LT to join them and the three of us on a design team planning a three-day off-site meeting of the entire LT. They agreed and invited Richard, head of safety, to join the design team.

Reflections

Establishing the enlarged design team is a very important success factor in our minds. We know that Robert, Ruby, and the LT need to feel ownership of the meeting and some sense of control in its execution. We also believe that they will bring important facts and feelings that will result in a much stronger design.

Richard has been with the organization for several years and has good rapport with other members of the LT and the broader organization.

In our first virtual meeting, we plan to establish norms on how the design team will work together.

We will use these meetings to jointly define outcomes, draft a design, and distribute roles for the off-site meeting.

Safe Environment

Ownership of the Learning

MAY 23: WE EXPAND THE INVOLVEMENT

We want to hear the questions and concerns that are on the mind of each member of the senior leadership team. So we asked Robert, Ruby, Richard, and all the other members of the LT individually to send us the key questions they think should be addressed by this executive team. We let them know that we will collect and use those questions to prepare a survey that all team members will answer individually. They seemed a bit surprised by this unusual request. I think they are more used to having an expert come in and ask questions rather than being asked to identify the questions they should be asked!

We explained that the answers to the set of questions would be captured via interviews with the three coaches and that the answers will be typed and distributed to the entire team. To generate openness and honest responses, the interview answers will be anonymous in the typed report.

Guided Reflection
Ownership of the Learning

Learning Coach
Just-in-Time Intervention

Reflections

We know some of the design team members feel they can read the pulse of the LT, but we are certain that the entire LT needs to be heard in advance of the meeting.

We know we're creating a bit of anxiety by not showing up as the "experts" who know what questions to ask in the survey. But by doing this, we are already providing participants the opportunity to reflect on their challenge and to engage in the process from the early stages. As important, we will create a more accurate diagnostic picture once they respond to these questions.

Our "expertise" comes in when we refine, edit, and add to the questions, and what counts is the timing of our input; it complements their tacit knowledge.

JUNE 27: WE ORGANIZE THE INFORMATION

Today we finished getting all the responses to the questionnaire. Respondents enjoyed the phone interviews and spoke candidly, while we took notes. We promised to organize their responses into an anonymous report so that everyone could see the other responses and evaluate the comments based on the merits of the ideas instead of on their feelings for the individual members. We will send them the interview summary a few days before the off-site meeting. This survey will provide invaluable information that we can use in the meeting.

Reflections

We sensed that LT members were excited by the chance to vent, to suggest ideas, and to articulate their hopes and fears with people who do not work inside the company.

Officially, the off-site meeting is still weeks away, but unofficially it has already begun with the interview process. By getting them to answer their own questions, we started the process whereby they would come up with their own solutions. We feel that self-doubt is already beginning to dissolve.

JULY 10: WORKING VIRTUALLY

We had another of our virtual design team meetings. The client company members seemed surprised by our insistence on establishing desired outcomes in so many dimensions (business, organizational, team, professional, and personal), but as they took some time to reflect, we jointly came up with a strong list of goals that we felt could be achieved in three days. See Table 2.

TABLE 2. **Desired Outcomes for the Off-Site Meeting**

DIMENSION	DESIRED OUTCOMES
Business dimension	■ Understand the context and business environment that affect the site and the changing needs ■ Start to develop a plan to engage the entire site ■ Define ways to build synergy and collaboration across functions
Organizational dimension	■ Exchange stories and capture learnings about how we have managed change successfully in the past ■ Develop strategies for addressing resistance to the change process ■ Refine and agree on the mission, vision, and strategy and key step for implementation, including roles and responsibilities
Team dimension	■ Understand the value of different perspectives and experience the power of cross-functional teamwork to create solutions for the challenge ■ Agree upon key team processes to improve efficiency (e.g., team norms, decision making) ■ Clarify roles and responsibilities for effecting change ■ Contract mutual expectations between team and leader
Professional dimension	■ Review and agree on leadership behaviors and skills that are needed to succeed in the new operating model ■ Learn new concepts and tools for leading change and transferring these concepts and tools to the appropriate functional teams ■ Practice new leadership behaviors and skills
Personal dimension	■ Become more appreciative of one another; learn about others' backgrounds, hopes, dreams, and concerns ■ Become more confident in our personal ability to lead the change throughout the organization

We have not yet distributed the collated responses to the questionnaires, but we tell our design team colleagues about the key trends, and this guides us in developing a workshop design that will respond to the stated urgent needs. The draft for the off-site session is coming along nicely. Everyone is giving input, we have a good dialogue going, and the diversity of the perspectives is making this a richer product. Spirits are high.

Reflections

Our way of organizing the design team sends a strong message to the LT about the importance of sharing decision making in this design process. We explained our reasons. Our intent is that they will take what they learn back to the workplace.

Balancing Task and Learning

Although we, the coaches, take primary responsibility for putting the final design together, everyone on the design team has a voice and veto power. We encourage everyone to speak up and we ensure active listening so everyone can learn about the different perspectives. It seems to be an empowering experience for them, too.

Learning Coach Learning Exchange

But certainly our design will change as other members of the LT put their fingerprints on it and we get into conversations that we cannot foresee. We have discussed this, so we are all anticipating changes to our design and are prepared to live with them.

Just-in-Time Intervention

The three of us are also mindful that shared leadership is one of the values Robert wants his team to adopt. So by sharing the leadership in our design team meetings, we inspire the other team members to ensure that everyone on the LT will have a role to play at the off-site meeting. This concept of shared leadership is one of the success factors that we will keep in mind throughout this project (1) within the consulting team, (2) within the design team, (3) within the LT, and (4) with the LT and the NLLT as they cascade the change throughout the rest of the organization.

Another important aspect of our planning process is the systemic approach to design. We are conscious of expanding our clients' thinking by asking for outcomes in several dimensions. They can easily see that the outcomes are interconnected and that it is possible and desirable to have outcomes in these five dimensions—since we are dealing with a system and each of these five dimensions contributes to a stronger whole.

The diagnostic process is a critical element in successful interventions, and the anonymous interviews often provide the most helpful input into the design.

Learning Coach

Five Dimensions System

Ownership of the Learning

SEPTEMBER 7: THE OFF-SITE MEETING

Today we finished the three-day off-site meeting with the LT. Ownership and expectations were high since the design team had kept the whole LT in the loop all through the planning. As they came in, having read the interview summary, all the LT members knew about the anonymous thoughts and feelings. The good news was that they saw the state of the site in a similar manner. The bad news was that the site is not in good shape. Morale is low, turnover is getting higher, productivity is down. We all had a lot of work to do!

But the team worked hard, and so did we. During these three days, team members papered the walls with their accomplishments and also captured the information on computers. A partial list of actions gives an indication of their explicit achievements. They developed the following:

- Hand drawings, with no words, from each person describing his or her important life events and interests as a means of getting to know one another better

- A set of norms for working together as a team over the three days and beyond

- Shared assumptions about the work for which they as the LT are responsible

- A prioritized list of the work, roles, and responsibilities they agreed should be delegated to the NLLT

- The mission of the LT and their vision of the site three years out

- *Myers-Briggs Type Indicator*® (MBTI®) assessment profiles of LT members, as a demonstration of their unique contributions to their team and as a reminder of the areas in which there are "gaps" in the team's preferred ways of behaving[11]

- Next steps defining who will do what by when

- An overview of the concepts and tools that we the coaches and team members have been introducing just in time during the course of the three days

- A preliminary design for the meeting with the NLLT in order to engage these managers in the change process

What was not on the walls but was equally important were the many conversations—formal and informal, in both large and small groups—that took place among members of the LT. We had several reflection and dialogue sessions during the three days, when we sat in a circle and just listened and talked without interrupting one another as together we made meaning of what we had just done and what we needed to do. We also captured the incidental learning that took place during break conversations and evening meals by taking periodic pauses and exchanging insights that the entire group might be interested in hearing. We organized a fun team-building exercise—but one with a serious intent—that served as a catalyst for articulating insights around change, resistance, trust, innovation, teamwork, and leadership. Just before the meeting ended, we asked who wanted to team with us as the new design team to prepare for the upcoming NLLT/LT meeting. Three other LT members quickly signed up.

Two individuals served as "hosts" for two of our evening meals, and they were responsible for designing focused questions for the whole team to explore and address at the table. This provided wonderful entertainment, with a lot of laughter, learning, and team bonding.

Reflections

Skillful debriefing of apparently lighthearted exercises can result in profound insights. Giving participants the challenging task of presenting significant life events and passions, using drawings but no words, had a substantial effect. First, it brought the team members together in a new way by letting them show hidden sides of their lives to people they thought they knew. Second, the drawings-only task, coming as it did within the first thirty minutes of the program, had the effect of getting participants to operate outside their normal comfort zones, which served to anticipate the potentially radical changes the site is facing in conducting its business in the future.

Holistic Involvement of the Individual

Linking

Many teams operate without ever taking the foundational step of agreeing how they want to work together and what members specifically expect from other members and from their leaders. Team members often have strong expectations about what they expect from other members, but because these remain tacit, the expectations end up creating frustrations. Members of this team have now established clearer contracts among themselves and have agreed on their norms and expectations by making explicit offers to, and requests of, one another.

Safe Environment

Feedback

One of the turning points during this meeting was reaching alignment on the assumptions that had to be true if "the site is going to be a world-famous, best-in-class, and operationally ex-

cellent facility." This was a very empowering session and gave everyone an opportunity to challenge the assumptions of the others, which led to a thorough review of company strengths and weaknesses and to the development of a common understanding of what will, in essence, be a new joint product.

During the meeting of the LT, Robert's personal assistant experienced a breakthrough. She had been invited to participate as an equal team member by Robert, who wanted the others to hear her thoughts and feelings because he values her perspective, insights, and long-term experience at the site. During the meeting, she made many poignant observations and asked challenging questions. It was no easy task for her to break out of her assumed support role. In our closing comments, she admitted that this had been the best leadership development experience she had ever had, as she received feedback from the LT that they truly valued her point of view.

Robert's deliberate invitation to his personal assistant sent a powerful message to the team and to the organization as a whole. It not only underscored the point that the LT must delegate responsibility and authority but also demonstrated his belief that insight and power come from many sources, especially if those sources are simply requested input and suggestions. He reasoned that the site needs the commitment and brainpower of every person in the plant.

Introducing the MBTI instrument was a good way to provide the leadership team with new insight into themselves as individuals and as a team. Once they were able to understand their own behavioral preferences and those of their teammates, they came to value the differences each brought to the team and became more appreciative of one another.

We had to keep in mind that the overall purpose of this intervention was to help team members define their future and at the same time learn how to install a participative culture that

Ownership of the Learning

Learning and Personality Styles

Linking

Guided Reflection

Learning Coach

Just-in-Time Intervention

Learning Exchange

Guided Reflection

Sequenced Learning

One-on-One Coaching Support

builds ownership of that vision. For that purpose, we aimed at transferring concepts, tools, and techniques to the LT, so that team members could, in turn, take the leading role in the following phases of the process. Therefore, it was very important to constantly show and explain what we, the Learning Coaches, were doing and why and to help LT members reflect on how they could introduce and apply the concepts, tools, and techniques with the next group, the NLLT.

The meeting location, with a spectacular view of the mountains, was a good setting for reflection. While paying attention to the task to be done within the assigned time frame, we made sure to allocate time for dialogue, informal exchanges, and reflection sessions. This is something unusual for most people who are working at a frantic pace in corporations, but it provided the best opportunities for making meaning, listening with undivided attention, exchanging perspectives and lessons, and deepening self-awareness. I think they all realized the power of these moments of slowing down and reflecting, enough to promote it themselves in the next meeting with the larger leadership group.

While the meeting ended on a high note, we know that when LT members return to work with their next steps and good intentions, they will be confronted by their on-the-job priorities. So we have decided to work with the new design team to find ways of maintaining the momentum while planning for the next meeting.

It will be important to offer support to Robert during this next interim period so that he feels he is able to support and encourage his team members in following through on their commitments.

SEPTEMBER 9:
WE GET READY FOR PHASE 2

Today we began planning for the second off-site meeting. Phase 2 will bring together the NLLT, a group of thirty leaders from the next management level, plus their personal assistants, with the LT acting as key facilitator of the event. We plan to prepare the assistants for active participation—helping them see themselves as more than "assistants" so that their voices will be heard; we'll also offer some preparatory support to LT members, helping them get ready for the new roles they will be playing during the off-site meeting.

Unfamiliar Environments

Reflections

There are two parallel streams in this cascading process, and we want to model the change the site must undergo. Just as it is essential for the LT to delegate power to the NLLT, who will serve as change agents, we, the coaches, must pass on to the LT the know-how and responsibility for running the change process. Our intent is to progressively step more to the side.

We want to offer our support in the pre-meeting phase, but the hope is that the LT will assume greater responsibility before and during the off-site meeting so that LT members are the ones to practice and apply what they have learned in the first meeting.

OCTOBER 24: WE SEND OUT
THE FIRST ASSIGNMENT

Following a process similar to the one we used with the LT, today we invited the forty-five participants in the upcoming off-site to get involved by reflecting on and responding to an electronic survey. We will collate the anonymous responses and send out the summary before the meeting. The responses will give us some additional ideas for the workshop design as well as insights into the feelings of the group.

NOVEMBER 8: WE PUT
THE FINAL TOUCHES ON THE DESIGN

We have now collated all the responses from the survey and sent them to participants. The participants are excited, many are optimistic and hopeful, but some are skeptical.

Reflections

We are aware of the mixed feelings. Within the LT, there is excitement; optimism related to eventually getting NLLT support; anger at some of the NLLT survey responses; and anxiety because of the limited time available to achieve all the desired outcomes. Team members feel positive because the timing is right and hopeful that we will succeed in getting alignment. Within the NLLT, there is both hope and skepticism. Among the personal assistants, there is apprehension that they will not be viewed as more than "just assistants" mingled with excitement at what will be for them a new level of participation. With this constellation of feelings, we need to be attentive to every detail in the planning but also be prepared to follow the flow and make our just-in-time interventions as appropriate.

Trust is not easy to generate, and simply telling people that coaches can be trusted is not enough. Even though we assured respondents that we, the coaches, would be the only ones to see the replies to the electronic survey, two respondents sent in their responses from a generic company e-mail address. Uncertain circumstances can lead to apprehension.

NOVEMBER 14:
WE BEGIN TOMORROW

There are two LT members who are not prepared for sessions they are leading. Their demanding work agendas didn't allow them to get ready as they wanted. In addition, one member of the LT has just joined the company, so he is new to the LT as well as to his own team.

Robert has expressed renewed willingness to take on a major cultural shift and leadership challenge.

Reflections

We realize the complexity of the systems we are engaged in: our client's systems (business, organizational, team, professional, and personal), our own team's similar systems, all the processes at play in each of the subsystems, the many emotions involved, the careers and reputations that will be affected, including our own, and the work itself—the tip of the iceberg below which everything else lies. We need to be mindful over the coming three days of the interactions of these different aspects and provide a safe space where they can be acknowledged.

We need to be alert to opportunities for providing just-in-time, one-on-one coaching support if we see participants with high stress levels or having difficulty.

The LT members will be acting as facilitators and coaches, applying some of the processes they experienced in the first off-site meeting. These roles will be a new challenge for them. This is an added concern because the survey replies focus strongly on the need for the LT to demonstrate clearer leadership, and we are aware that every member of the LT will be facing leadership credibility challenges personally and collectively in the upcoming meeting.

Five Dimensions System

One-on-One Coaching Support

Unfamiliar Environments

NOVEMBER 15:
WE HAVE QUITE A START

This was an intense day! It started in a powerful way, when Robert opened the meeting with a warm, personal, clear, and compelling message: We're all leaders; we're all accountable; in the next couple of days, we have the opportunity and the responsibility to speak up and participate; the future is in our hands.

The design was definitely interactive and supported this aim. We established meeting norms, heard everyone's expectations for the workshop, and divided the group into four cross-functional subteams to allow for more personal introductions. Getting to know one another aided in creating a better atmosphere, which proved to be very helpful for other interactions during the day. The reflection and dialogue session gave everyone the opportunity to find his or her voice in what became a rich conversation about team members' shared challenges.

Then the tension rose after LT members presented the vision and mission they had developed. When NLLT members were given a chance to share their reactions, their criticism was straight and to the point—the presentation of the LT was flat, lacking energy, passion, and conviction; the mission and vision were not compelling.

We saw this as a sign that people are taking Robert's request seriously and are speaking their minds. They are engaged. But the LT was happy neither with the reaction nor with its own performance. We coaches discussed the day's events with some LT members individually and reflected on the value of NLLT members being willing and able to say what they think and feel. This, after all, is the culture the LT is trying to create—a culture of engagement.

Tomorrow will be an important day. We all need an evening off to reflect on all the events of today.

> ### Reflections
>
> *How important it was to create a safe environment, where individuals could express themselves without fear of being blamed or judged—at least publicly!*
>
> *The individual support we offered just in time also helped the LT overcome some hurdles. It is key to be "on our toes," alert to the need and opportunities for offering support.*

Safe Environment

One-on-One Coaching Support

Just-in-Time Intervention

NOVEMBER 16: THE LT PLANS THE NEXT STEPS

This morning, before the opening session of the day, we met with the LT to see what, if any, changes we should make. Some members of the LT were still quite angry with some of the feedback they had received the day before, and it took some time to calm them down and help them see the silver lining in the thunderclouds. We encouraged them to hold on to their anger and remain open to feedback if possible, with a smile and a thank-you. How else could a participative atmosphere be promoted? Robert had been reflecting on what had happened and believes that one of the things that was missing was a full disclosure of the site's financial situation. He felt it was time to raise the curtain. His instincts were absolutely right.

His thirty-minute, off-the-cuff presentation using a marker and a flip-chart to illustrate a few points turned the meeting around. Now LT members understood the rationale and need for a transformational change. They were ready to roll up their sleeves and work.

And work they did! We introduced an organizational diagnostic tool and let group members select which part of the organization they wanted to analyze. They worked in small groups and presented their recommendations, getting further input from the large group. Most of the recommendations were converted into decisions with clear next steps stating who was going to do what by when. Energy was high. They made visible progress.

Another highlight of the day was the session clarifying the roles and responsibilities of the LT and the NLLT. Each group took some time to identify what it needed and wanted from the other. They presented their requests and offers, and after some questions both groups were able to adopt the other's offers augmented by their respective requests. By clarifying the work and the expectations a bit more, both groups will feel empowered.

But the most unexpected by-product was the role the personal assistants played. Some new members of the NLLT and the LT and one member of the consulting team couldn't tell who the personal assistants were, because all were interacting as leaders! They lived up to Robert's request and made valuable observations and asked good questions. On the final evening, Robert's personal assistant was the host at one of the tables and facilitated a fascinating conversation over dinner, keeping everyone engaged. A bystander would have thought she was the company president by the way she handled herself!

The meeting ended with a perfect touch, as Robert role-modeled a new behavior: He asked the group to take a moment for reflection beyond the tangible accomplishments and identify what had made this meeting work. By doing so, he underscored the value of extracting and exchanging learnings.

Reflections

As we debriefed our meeting as a consulting team, we reflected on the many factors that contributed to its success. They are a combination of ARL elements and good OD practices:

- **The power of an invitation.** *Robert invited members of his extended team to speak up, and they did; however, the ground* *rules contributed to creating a safe environment that allowed people to take risks. Several of the NLLT members commented on how important it was that the LT listened to their feedback and criticism without defensiveness.*

- **The power of awareness.** *Robert's financial disclosure opened the eyes of the NLLT and set the stage for productive teamwork.*

- **The power of process.** *We introduced several practical instruments and tools that were enabling and empowering.*

- **The power of sharing power.** *It began with us, the "expert" coaches, inviting LT members to take on our roles. They, in turn, empowered the NLLT, which now feels recognized and has a substantial role that is clearly defined.*

- **The power of listening.** *The LT made one of the strongest impressions on NLLT members by listening to them.*

- **The power of speaking up.** *Many NLLT members and the personal assistants spoke up with passion and clarity and were given applause and verbal appreciation by their colleagues.*

- **The power of recognition and appreciation.** *The coaches and the LT were conscious of looking for appropriate times to say "Thank you" and "Good job."*

- **The power of feedback.** *We took time to give one another feedback on a just-in-time, end-of-day basis. We saw changes in behavior among the LT and the NLLT as a result of feedback we gave them and they gave each other.*

- **The power of role-modeling.** *We and the LT were conscious of walking the talk. It wasn't always easy, but we supported one another in doing our best, knowing that many eyes were looking to see if we really believed what we said.*

- **The power of teamwork.** *Together we were much stronger than we were individually, and as a united delivery team with*

Safe Environment
Ownership of the Learning

Just-in-Time Intervention

Learning Coach
Ownership of the Learning

Appreciative Approach

Feedback

> *the LT, the power was multiplied. The LT had a similar real-ization when team members felt the energy flow between them and the NLLT; they became an electromagnetic field.*
>
> - ***The power of hard work and planning.*** *We became very aware that all the hours of sharing, listening, interviewing, analyzing, meeting, designing, redesigning, coaching, facili-tating, presenting, and evaluating made a difference.*

JANUARY 5:
TAKING FULL OWNERSHIP

Today we had a phone conversation with the new design team, a combination of two LT and two NLLT members. As we stepped into phase 3, they are taking full ownership in designing an up-coming meeting, the first of new quarterly meetings of the com-bined LT and NLLT—a decision made in the last off-site workshop. The purpose of these meetings will be to address current chal-lenges collectively and in subgroups and at the same time practice the new behaviors and processes they have been learning. They also need to get ready for rolling the change throughout the rest of the organization.

We coached them in getting clear outcomes in the design they are planning and encouraged them to engage different partici-pants during the different sections of the meeting. It was exciting to find that they had already planned for several reflection and dialogue sessions.

JANUARY 31:
WORKING AS A SHADOW COACH

Today one member of our team served as a "shadow coach" for the design team during the combined LT/NLLT group meeting.

The design team did a superb job of facilitating the meeting. Team members applied many of the ARL elements and used several tools they had acquired during the previous two meetings. They worked as a team and called on their shadow coach to step in on only one occasion, when they felt a bit out of their depth. But the meeting was the venue for a demonstration of courageous commitment to a new challenge by the entire leadership team. Robert made a presentation in which he indicated that the company CEO had told all offices that they had to make financial cutbacks. The group of forty-five stunned people, after initial reluctance, proposed a reflection and dialogue session, after which they broke up into four subgroups; the subgroups proposed painful headcount reductions along with other creative ways of saving money.

> ## Reflections
>
> *A shadow coach plays a supportive role as an individual or a team transitions from awareness to mastery. A shadow coach may offer quick insights, provide timely feedback, and, if necessary, take hold of the steering wheel. Pilots learn how to fly with a shadow pilot at their side. And most athletes have coaches who sit on the sidelines, take notes, and provide instructive feedback.*
>
> *The team showed, in only its second meeting, that it was prepared. It used new tools, processes, and behaviors when facing substantial challenges.*

MOVING FORWARD

We are discussing with Robert and Ruby how to design their combined leadership meetings so that the meetings become professional development opportunities as well as business development planning sessions. In such a scenario, we will be working as shadow coaches as well as instructors, instilling the skill sets they have identified as necessary as they engage the rest of the organization in the change process.

> ### Reflections
>
> *We feel happy with the developments we see. We know that keeping up the momentum will not be easy. Robert, Ruby, the LT, and the NLLT are aware that the work is not over. Yet they understand the ARL principles and elements, and they have the necessary tools to continue the work. Their transformation is a work in progress. As a Chinese proverb says, "A garden is never finished."*

SUMMING UP

In this section, which concludes with this story from the pages of a diary, you were able to follow the movements, thoughts, and hesitations of a Learning Coach in action. You have been shown the ARL elements embedded in the stories. But what are these elements anyway? What logic, if any, brings together all these different components? Where does this all come from? Is this a new approach or an eclectic collection of old wisdom?

In the next section, you will find some answers to these, and more, questions.

▼

PART FOUR

Reflecting on the Action

In this section, we reflect on the ARL action. So far, you have journeyed with us through applications of ARL and seen how this process works in many different environments for many different participants. In previous chapters, we inserted (just in time) the ARL elements as they surfaced in each case. We wanted to show in an organic way how the elements constituted the backbone of the interventions. At the end of chapters 2 and 3, we gave brief definitions of the elements and explained how the elements were included using specific tools or processes. In later chapters, we only listed the elements that were highlighted in the stories. And you saw how a Learning Coach works.

But *why* does ARL work so well? What is the foundation of this practice? What are the principles that lie behind the choices of tools and processes and that ground the results? In this section, we present the history and conceptual framework of ARL and delve deeper into the role of the ARL coach, also known simply as Learning Coach. We show the journey that led from the empirical real-life practice of ARL to conceptualizing the sixteen elements of ARL. We also present the underlying assumptions that make those elements so powerful.

Chapter 9 is a brief history of the evolution of ARL. In chapter 10, you will find a detailed description of the sixteen elements and their implementation in the different stages of a learning intervention. Chapters 11 and 12 give you the pedagogical assumptions behind the elements and the theoretical underpinnings that support ARL-based interventions. Here we present the ten learning principles, rooted in a variety of disciplines, that are the conceptual foundation of ARL. Chapter 13 describes in depth the different roles of a Learning Coach, a specialized facilitator who designs and implements ARL programs.

Ready? Let's begin.

CHAPTER 9

Origins and Evolution of ARL

The roots of Action Reflection Learning can be traced to the management training practices of the 1970s or, more specifically, to a quiet revolt against those practices led by a group of visionary Swedish professors, researchers, and consultants in business and the behavioral sciences.[12] We will follow the path of ARL as it evolved organically, led by practitioners adapting to new and challenging contexts.

MANAGEMENT DEVELOPMENT IN THE 1970S

In the 1970s, corporations were led by technically savvy managers who had attended management training programs based on the traditional business school model. Their training consisted mostly of lectures given by theoretically grounded professors who imparted their knowledge in the different administrative areas. Cases were occasionally used to exemplify the concepts and to challenge the thinking of the students, although they were not very effective in developing application skills.

The educational setting replicated the power structure of the corporate world. On one side was the expert, teacher, or manager, who had the knowledge and expertise, who knew all the answers, who directed, indicated, instructed, and supervised. On the other side sat "tabula rasa" individuals, students or employees, who were expected to listen, imitate, follow instructions, and execute.

The philosopher Ivan Illich presents an interesting perspective of the context of the 1970s. Illich describes teachers as a particular group of experts, who reinforced the system by making students believe that they, the teachers, were the only ones entitled to define and certify knowledge and learning. As a consequence, individuals were supposed to learn only from those experts within their conceptual and institutional framework.[13]

Looking at that classroom from today's perspective, we would see that something is not quite right. Why did the educators, who were teaching managers with actual and current experience in management, deal with them as if their experience and business know-how were of little account? Surely these managers had gathered considerable wisdom through their experience that could be used. Why was that knowledge left out of the classroom? How applicable to the participants' reality was the content of the lectures? Were those concepts and theories transferable, or was there tacit acceptance of a gap between theory and practice that was simply being ignored or denied? What were the real challenges those participants had to face, and how did the lectures address them? Whose needs were being served by these lectures? The lecturer's ego needs or the participants' needs for a "certificate"? And what did the certificates certify? Attendance or learning? Was memorizing the same as learning? What did management development mean in those days? A key skill of managers is the ability to manage people. How did the technical instruction teach managers to be better people managers?

Illich points out that some adult educators began to see themselves as part of a countercultural movement, the management training equivalent of a New Left that pushed for participatory development.[14] He characterized the alternative framework offered by the new thinkers as four oppositions:

- Learning, as opposed to schooling

- Conviviality, as opposed to manipulation

- "Responsibilization," as opposed to "deresponsibilization"

- Participation, as opposed to control

These characteristics seem to be part of the foundation of ARL.

PRECEDING ARL: THE MIL MODEL

In the late 1970s, a group of professors at the University of Lund, Sweden, met with friends in management positions and colleagues working as consultants and HR professionals in Swedish organizations. What brought them together was their frustration with the way training programs offered by educational institutions were addressing the professional development of executives. They wanted to create a movement of protest against the prevailing approaches and methods used in professional management training.

Their ambition was first to focus on developing leadership competencies—instead of management competencies, such as finance, marketing, or strategy.[15] For that, they analyzed the contents of what was being taught to managers and questioned whether the syllabi actually served to develop leadership.[16] They realized that developing the skills of enlightened leadership depended less on memorizing facts and theories and more on learning new behaviors and attitudes.

Behaviors are the visible expressions of attitudes, beliefs, and values. Scandinavia has a history of strongly participative and democratic movements. The professors and consultants gathered at Lund saw contradictions between Scandinavian values and beliefs and the way corporations managed employees. Are managers supposed to use authority or advocacy? Are supervision and control their only responsibilities, or is management more about empowerment and delegation? How do expertise and the power that comes with it interface with consensus? These questions showed the Lund group that developing new behaviors was closely connected with both reviewing the values and assumptions underlying the current leadership practices and uncovering contradictions and paradoxes.

Next, they explored the question of what would be the most appropriate process or method for the new developmental goals. It was clear that the answer went beyond teaching and lecturing, which were inadequate for current leadership requirements. They realized that they had to find what would enhance *learning* for the individuals.

They posited that education for this type of leadership had to be based on, and contain, an experiential component. It also had to be relevant and connected in a pragmatic way to the challenges individuals were facing in their organizations. Managers had to develop new answers to new questions that were arising from their daily work. Enough of indoctrination in the theories of others; learning was about developing their own theories while solving current dilemmas as well as gaining new perspectives and mindsets for approaching strategic issues in their leadership roles. It was about what managers had to know as much as how they had to act and be, with themselves and with others in daily organizational contexts. If what mattered was learning how to behave and think differently, the classical teaching model was not suited to this purpose.

This avant-garde group came up with a different way of training that focused on learning rather than on teaching. And its members developed their new way of training by asking themselves a number of questions: How can we leverage our own collective experience? How do we solve this educational challenge? How do we find a pragmatic solution? How do we, as educators, change the way we think, review our assumptions and belief systems, uncover our values, and address the paradoxes of our educator's role?

This is how the MiL (Management in Lund) Institute came into being.[17] In 1976, the initial group brought together about one hundred professionals from the corporate world, consulting organizations, and universities to work in a participative way to develop concepts upon which the new approach would be based. Over a period of eighteen months, MiL members conceived programs that would be based on three key principles: (1) develop leaders who could thrive on change and were comfortable living with ambiguity and uncertainty; (2) build trusting relationships; and (3) develop learning based on action and reflection, using real-time interventions on current challenges. MiL brought together groups of managers to work on real, organizationally significant projects.

THE EVOLUTION OF THE MIL MODEL INTO ACTION REFLECTION LEARNING

In the 1980s, MiL designed and implemented programs to develop value-based leadership, using a design in which learning was based on taking action to tackle real-life organizational issues. This model was very similar to the Action Learning approach developed by Reginald Revans in the 1940s, in which a group of people met periodically to solve problems related to work. As it was described by Revans in those days, individuals brought their own problems, and group members asked questions that helped those individuals find their own answers.[18]

Action Learning programs differed from the MiL model in the 1980s in that MiL used facilitators, called "project team advisors" (later renamed "Learning Coaches").[19] Revans advised against the use of facilitators, recommending that the groups be self-managed through rotating leadership. Furthermore, MiL used strategic group projects rather than projects related to the problems of individuals as the arena for learning, and the sessions were of variable duration.

This was just the beginning. The MiL model continued to evolve organically, shaped by organizational needs, restrictions, and special requests and driven by the participants' context and expectations.[20] Practitioners within and outside of Scandinavia used their creativity and best professional judgment to stay loyal to the grounding principles of using real challenges and alternating action with reflection as a way of developing new mind-sets, attitudes, and behaviors appropriate for times of uncertainty. Applying the experiential and reflective learning mode to themselves, practitioners experimented by altering the number and duration of sessions, the type of projects selected, and the role of the Learning Coach and the style of his or her interventions. As the approach evolved and developed characteristics that no longer fit the original Action Learning settings and specifications, the practitioners named it Action Reflection Learning.[21]

NEW PROFILE, NEW APPLICATIONS

ARL began to be applied in a diversity of contexts. In the academic environment, ARL was used for an executive development program at the master's level for graduates of the University of Lund and as the teaching methodology for a postgraduate program at the University of Belgrano, Argentina.

The program's outcomes also began to transcend its initial leadership development purpose of converting managers into leaders. ARL was used for a number of other purposes that had one goal in common: Something had to be learned. Examples of the expanded use of ARL include the following:

- Helping individuals learn to work together as part of a post-merger integration

- Learning how to create new business strategies
- Helping teams learn how to handle a conflict or crisis situation
- Providing a process for coaching individuals
- Developing high-performing teams
- Helping a leader transition from one team to the next
- Preparing young talent for upcoming challenges
- Developing mentoring programs
- Designing organizational change programs
- Developing specific competencies
- Developing leader-coaches
- Learning how to implement performance appraisal processes
- Developing synergy in regional teams
- Designing meetings and conferences
- Developing Learning Coaches

By expanding the application of its approach to new contexts and contents, ARL moved naturally beyond the original focus. It transitioned from an approach to supporting leadership development to a learning methodology. Consistent with ARL's constructivist essence, the practice continued to evolve naturally, led by practitioners, not driven by theories or the conceptual frameworks of others.

As more practitioners used ARL, participants and newcomers asked, "What exactly is ARL?" This was a difficult question to answer, as the development of the ARL approach had occurred in opposition to theories and concepts that were transmitted as universal truths. ARL was deeply rooted in an experiential learning model that explicitly invited individuals to create their own interpretations and versions of "truth." For example, at the beginning of some programs, each participant received a hardcover book titled *Leadership*. But upon opening it, the participant would find that all the pages were blank. This sent the following message: "Whatever you learn about leadership will be your own creation. You will define what leadership is for you."

This didn't mean that participants were left without guidance on how to articulate their reflected experiences, but it did mean that the "learning" in ARL was the responsibility of participants, who should put their new insights into words, thus making the learnings communicable and transferable to other situations. And participants were invited to develop their theories and insights by interacting with others, not by studying in solitude.

NAME IT TO SHARE IT

The lack of a conceptual framework defining the boundaries of ARL was consistent with its underlying values, by which truth is defined by each individual rather than taught by experts. If these are the values at the foundation of ARL, how would it be conceivable to define ARL—what it is, what it is not, how it should be applied? Who would put himself or herself into such a position of authority?

However, it becomes very difficult to share and transfer knowledge when we cannot describe what we do and explain the tacit logic behind the interventions. Some practitioners wrote about their experiences; some scholars analyzed the process, the results, and the roles played by the different actors; and a group of practitioners drafted a list of characteristics and core components used in ARL interventions and the skills required to implement the approach.[22] This meant that it was possible to make a distinction between trusting individuals to learn by reflecting on their experiences (avoiding the traditional teaching approach) and shaping a methodology that would help individuals learn. The challenge remained, up to this day, to walk the fine line between being creatively organic and establishing frameworks that allow sharing knowledge. Yet the question "What actually *is* ARL?" inspired Isabel Rimanoczy to conduct the research with ARL practitioners that led to the first coding of ARL practice.[23]

SUMMING UP

Conceptual frameworks are like construction-site scaffoldings. They allow us to continue building, connecting what is already there with what will be there next. Through conceptual frameworks, it is possible to transfer knowledge, to build upon others' experiences, and to critique, improve, and continue building the practice. Yet the practice remains the main stage of ARL, as reflection and learning evolve from the reality of the action.

With this insight into the origins and evolution of ARL, and having journeyed with us through the stories we shared with you in preceding chapters, you are ready to dive into the what and why of ARL. What is the rationale behind these elements with which you are now familiar? What do they mean exactly? When and how can they be put into action? The next chapter sheds some light on these questions.

CHAPTER 10

Elements of the ARL Practice

Despite the expanded implementation of ARL-based programs in the United States, Latin America, Europe, and Asia, little research about the practice is available.[24] In 2004, Isabel Rimanoczy initiated a qualitative exploratory study to identify the principles and elements common to ARL practitioners. After reviewing the existing literature, she determined that what were described as characteristics of ARL interventions constituted a combination of components at different levels of abstraction, ranging from concrete tools, such as a learning journal a practitioner would use, to abstract concepts, such as the idea of reflection as key to learning.

With the support of Dr. Boris Drizin, Rimanoczy established an initial nomenclature organizing the components into three categories: (1) what seemed to be common elements in ARL interventions, (2) principles underlying the elements, and (3) specific processes or tools and resources used by ARL practitioners. The study included a questionnaire sent out to thirty-three practitioners who had participated in the design or implementation of two or more ARL-based programs between 1995 and 2004 as well as selected interviews. The sample covered a wide geographic spread: Sweden, Denmark, the United Kingdom, Mexico, Argentina, Chile, Peru, Colombia, and the United States.[25]

The study's findings resulted in a list of elements that were consistently used by 98 percent of the surveyed practitioners. Further analysis of the elements allowed Rimanoczy to identify some of the assumptions on which they were grounded, which then led to establishment of the underlying theoretical frameworks that supported and probably were responsible for the impact of the approach.

THE ELEMENTS OF ACTION REFLECTION LEARNING

ARL elements constitute the core characteristics that, when implemented together, distinguish ARL interventions from other types of learning interventions that may include some of the elements. An element is not a process in itself, but it is at the core of different tools or activities selected by the Learning Coach. ARL is identified by sixteen elements, fifteen of which are grouped into three clusters around one central element, the Learning Coach, as outlined below and illustrated in Figure 3.

Elements related to *what* the Learning Coach does:

- Feedback
- Guided Reflection
- Learning Exchange
- Linking
- One-on-One Coaching Support

Elements related to *how* the Learning Coach creates the setting:

- Appreciative Approach
- Balancing Task and Learning
- Five Dimensions System

FIGURE 3. **Map of the Sixteen ARL Elements**

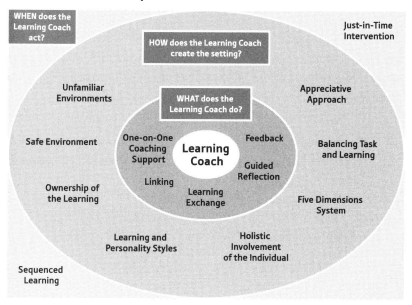

- Holistic Involvement of the Individual

- Learning and Personality Styles

- Ownership of the Learning

- Safe Environment

- Unfamiliar Environments

Elements related to *when* the Learning Coach acts:

- Just-in-Time Intervention

- Sequenced Learning

The central element:

- Learning Coach

ARL ELEMENTS AND THE STAGES OF LEARNING

We have identified five stages in learning situations and mapped out the location of ARL elements in each stage (see Table 3).[26] The five stages are:

- **Discovery:** the initial contact with the learners and/or the client requesting a training event. The purpose of the discovery is to establish the learning needs and expectations.

- **Planning:** the process of mapping out resources and contents, logistics, time frame, communication, participants, budget, staffing, materials, and evaluation processes.

- **Design and redesign:** the selection of specific learning activities and methods, techniques, and sequence to be implemented. The design occurs prior to the first learning session, and redesign occurs during and throughout the learning sessions in response to emerging needs.

- **Learning interventions:** the specific interventions of the Learning Coach during the learning sessions. The interventions could be undertaken to introduce a tool or a concept, to give instructions for an activity, to offer feedback or individual coaching support, to work on facilitation roles, to foster reflection, and so on.

- **Evaluation and debrief:** the processes designed to assess achievement of expected outcomes and learning goals as well as feedback to the Learning Coach about the results of the overall event. This occurs informally during the sessions and, often in a more formal, structured way, at the end of individual modules and at the end of the learning event. These inputs are analyzed and processed to incorporate improvements.

TABLE 3. **ARL Elements and Stages of Learning**

ARL ELEMENT	STAGES OF LEARNING					
	Discovery	Planning	Design and Redesign	Learning Interventions	Evaluation and Debrief	
Feedback						WHAT
Guided Reflection						
Learning Exchange						
Linking						
One-on-one Coaching Support						
Appreciative Approach						HOW
Balancing Task and Learning						
Five Dimensions System						
Holistic Involvement of the Individual						
Learning and Personality Styles						
Ownership of the Learning						
Safe Environment						
Unfamiliar Environments						
Just-in-Time Intervention						WHEN
Sequenced Learning						
Learning Coach						WHO

ELEMENTS RELATED TO *WHAT* THE LEARNING COACH DOES

Learning Coaches facilitate or implement these ARL elements.

Element: Feedback

What is it?

Feedback provides increased awareness of how one's words and actions affect others, both positively and negatively.

When is it applied?

Discovery	Planning	Design and Redesign	Learning Interventions	Evaluation and Debrief

Feedback is an important element guiding the organic redesign throughout the learning interventions, as it allows the Learning Coach to monitor how the needs and interests of the participants are being met and to adjust and correct the plan accordingly.

It is also present during learning interventions, for the purpose of helping learners to see themselves through the eyes of others and to increase their awareness. Finally, this element is the core of the evaluation and debrief.

How is it applied?

The coach implements feedback through pauses and general questions; voting processes; Stop, Reflect, Write, Report processes; and written questionnaires.

For the benefit of learners, feedback can be implemented through fishbowl exercises, in which one or several persons sit in the center of a circle and share feedback while other participants sit in the outside circle and listen actively to the conversation; team dialogue sessions; specific questions; skits in which individuals act on their perceptions of others' behaviors; one-on-one conversations; learning partnerships, in which two individuals agree to help each other learn by giving each other feedback; learning exchanges in formal or informal settings; toasting ceremonies; and individual reflection.

Element: Guided Reflection

What is it?

This refers to directing learners toward reflection. Guided reflection draws the learning out of the experience by creating awareness of connections and possible cause–effect relationships as well as opportunities to transfer that knowledge into other contexts.

When is it applied?

Discovery	Planning	Design and Redesign	Learning Interventions	Evaluation and Debrief

This element has a relevant role in the discovery and design phases as well as throughout the learning interventions of a Learning Coach. Evaluation and debriefing sessions also include this element.

How is it applied?

The Learning Coach may implement this element through pauses and general questions; the Stop, Reflect, Write, Report technique;[27] writing assignments; journaling; dialogue sessions; visualization exercises; learning partners; and group exchange sessions. The allocation of time, the careful preparation of a conducive setting, a focus, and an appropriate medium are the key components of every method used for implementing guided reflection. Activities using symbolic triggers—such as images, poetry, movies, drawings, collages, or other artistic expressions—are also useful instruments for generating guided reflection in that they respect participants' different levels of awareness or ability to express themselves through words.

Element: Learning Exchange

What is it?

Participants are encouraged to share their experiences, reflections, and insights with others, so that they will understand that others have perspectives and worldviews that are very different from their own. This awareness, in turn, promotes critical thinking and encourages participants to examine their own assumptions and mental models.

When is it applied?

Discovery	Planning	Design and Redesign	Learning Interventions	Evaluation and Debrief

When ARL-based practitioners draft a learning design, they pay special attention to providing multiple opportunities for exchanging learnings. Throughout the learning interventions, participants periodically regroup in order to create different learning exchange scenarios.

Finally, on occasion the Learning Coach may share the collected evaluations with the group, which, by enabling exchange of learnings, gives everybody a chance to hear what others have found valuable, important, or disturbing.

How is it applied?

This element is implemented through a variety of processes or tools. Depending on the number of participants involved in the exchange, they could be assigned, randomly or intentionally, to work in duos, trios, or small groups. Large-group dialogue sessions are effective in allowing everyone's voice to be heard. The learning exchange can be implemented in homogeneous groups, diverse groups, affinity groupings, and rotating groups, using, for example, the World Café technique.[28] It could happen through assignments such as peer coaching, learning partners, presentations, and reports. Other processes relate to the setting: walk-and-talk sessions, fishbowl exercises, posters, open space, flip-chart postings, and virtual discussion boards.

Element: Linking

What is it?

Linking helps build a bridge between the event and other situations, creating generalizations. When we generalize learning, we are able to disconnect it from the situation and consider other situations in which it could be applied. For example, when we have a conflict with a person because we didn't clarify our mutual expectations, we can extract the learning that we should have stated our expectations from the beginning. To generalize this learning means that we could consider setting expectations in other situations, too, with other people. When what is being learned can be connected to other contexts, it expands the application and usefulness of the learning beyond the immediate concerns or issues.

When is it applied?

Discovery	Planning	Design and Redesign	Learning Interventions	Evaluation and Debrief

An important task for the Learning Coach is to make periodic connections between what is being learned and discussed, the reality of the learners, and the overall topic. The evaluations, whether formative or summative, should also include questions that invite learners to consider how they will apply and transfer what was learned to other contexts.

How is it applied?

This element is implemented through processes such as offers directed to the learners (e.g., "You could also use this decision-making process with your family"); through Stop, Reflect, Write, Report (e.g., "Take a moment and respond to this question: What are the takeaways from this morning?"); through suggestion of intentional connections (e.g., "I was thinking that if we had conducted this decision-making process yesterday, our conversation would have been much easier—so you see it can also be used in large groups"); and through exercises that invite learners to establish connections between what was done or learned and other scenarios in which it could be applied (e.g., grouping individuals in dyads to exchange the conclusions they extract and how they could apply them during the following week).

In evaluations, linking is implemented through processes such as the Critical Incident question, which asks participants to identify how they connect the highs and lows of the session with other environments. Reflection and dialogue sessions can also focus on establishing these connections.

Element: One-on-One Coaching Support

What is it?

This element refers to giving learners both formal and informal individual coaching support.

When is it applied?

Discovery	Planning	Design and Redesign	Learning Interventions	Evaluation and Debrief

Individual support is included in the discovery and design phases, by allocating time for individual coaching sessions in initial contacts with learners, and during the learning sessions. Depending on the type of learning context, postsession contacts could be valuable, and the Learning Coach could conduct individual debriefing conversations with those learners who are interested.

How is it applied?

The coach implements this element by establishing a personal connection with the learner, before the learning events, in order to collect expectations, interests, and needs. Launching a personal relationship with the learner is key. The coach can take opportunities to touch base with participants during the learning sessions, in the informal moments of check-in, during breaks, or when finalizing a session. Informal support is given through specific questions, such as by inquiring how the person is feeling, how she is meeting her needs, what has been challenging, and so on.

In some cases, the coach may provide more formal one-on-one support via coaching sessions or less structured e-mail follow-up.

ELEMENTS RELATED TO *HOW* THE LEARNING COACH CREATES THE SETTING

Learning Coaches apply these ARL elements in creating environments for learning.

Element: Appreciative Approach

What is it?

This refers to promoting an atmosphere of mutual recognition and acceptance and fostering empowerment. The Learning Coach demonstrates this element by valuing strengths, supporting self-directed improvements, and trusting the participants' abilities to address problems and challenges.

When is it applied?

Discovery	Planning	Design and Redesign	Learning Interventions	Evaluation and Debrief

The appreciative approach runs throughout the whole learning process, from the initial discovery phase to the evaluation and debrief phase.

How is it applied?

During the needs assessment, it is important that the coach pay attention to the political agendas that may be in play, especially those representing interests other than the interests of participants. At this stage, it is valuable to listen carefully for expectations that relate to punitive, evaluative, or judging outcomes.

In the planning and design phases, the appreciative approach is manifested in the planning sequence for activities, starting with giving participants an opportunity to contribute as a way of appreciating their knowledge and moving toward a content that honors their interests and knowledge.

The coach indicates the appreciative approach in learning interventions through comments that value all contributions and respect the diverse voices, through body language and caring gestures and through responses that show tolerance, patience, and interest in understanding. The coach must be the role model for the larger audience and, for example, should take time to paraphrase or reframe hostile comments into more appreciative terms.

Activities such as certain feedback processes, pauses that recognize achievements, celebrations, rotating toasts, gift giving, and speech writing foster appreciation.

Element: Balancing Task and Learning

What is it?

This refers to giving equal attention to progress on the task (the content) and to the learning (the process).

When is it applied?

Discovery	Planning	Design and Redesign	Learning Interventions	Evaluation and Debrief

This element is important during the discovery phase. If participants are focused only on "learning," it is important to invite them to consider task-related outcomes. And if task is the only focus, then the challenge is to find the learning opportunities that could be hiding there, ready to be discovered.

During the planning and design phases, the Learning Coach should allocate time to both the task at hand and to the lessons to be extracted. And finally, the coach is responsible for ensuring that participants maintain awareness of this balance. Such negotiations may pose a challenge, because participants will naturally focus more intensely on the task at hand than on the learning to be extracted.

How is it applied?

This element is implemented through pauses and general questions as well as writing activities using journals or logs. Dialogue sessions are a valuable process for creating space for making meaning and extracting lessons, as are learning partners, writing assignments, and activities that include symbolic expression through drawing, collage, image interpretation, or other artistic means.

Element: Five Dimensions System

What is it?

In order to generate lasting learning, the Learning Coach should consider five dimensions in the design, delivery, and evaluation of any learning intervention (see Figure 4):

- **The business dimension:** the real problem, business, or challenge on which the learning is anchored

- **The organizational dimension:** the larger system, company, or organization to which the participants belong

- **The professional dimension:** the competencies that need to be learned

FIGURE 4. **The Five Dimensions System of ARL**

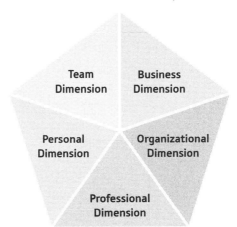

- **The personal dimension:** the attitudes and mind-sets that need to be developed so that the competencies can be converted into action

- **The team dimension:** the processes and dynamics that individuals use to work together

Although some of these dimensions relate to individuals and some to larger groups such as the organization or the team, the system is not a hierarchy: the coach is often working in all five dimensions at once.

When is it applied?

Discovery	Planning	Design and Redesign	Learning Interventions	Evaluation and Debrief

The Five Dimensions System is present throughout the ARL-based intervention, from the discovery phase and establishment of outcomes, throughout the design and learning intervention phases, to the evaluation and debrief phase.

How is it applied?

In the discovery phase, the coach specifically collects information that covers potential outcomes or needs in the five different dimensions. This information may not be provided in a direct way, but it could be inferred and constructed, organizing data into these categories.

In the planning phase, the coach uses the systemic perspective to ensure that the larger system is involved, be it through stakeholders or through processes that support the event. For example, in the case of a workshop to be held in an educational setting, the coach makes sure that the organization communicates the right message to potential participants, using the appropriate timing and media.

For the design phase, the selection of activities ensures that the different dimensions are well represented. A number of questions need to be asked: Are the competencies addressed in any of the sessions? What are the attitudes that need to be developed for the skills? How will learners connect those skills with the teamwork? What challenges will anchor the learning?

The learning interventions are integrated throughout the design in order to address the outcomes identified in the five dimensions. The evaluations likewise measure the results in these five dimensions.

Finally, during the debrief, analysis of the evaluations also covers the five dimensions.

Element: Holistic Involvement of the Individual

What is it?

This refers to the special effort the Learning Coach makes to engage the "total" learner—intellectually, emotionally, spiritually, and physically.

When is it applied?

Discovery	Planning	Design and Redesign	Learning Interventions	Evaluation and Debrief

This element occurs during the planning and design phases, in order to accommodate activities and time for the different levels of engagement. Learning interventions also pay attention to the holistic involvement of the learners, and the evaluation should solicit cognitive and emotional responses.

How is it applied?

During the planning phase, it is important to explore the natural tendencies of a group of learners, given organizational, cultural, thematic, or other conditions. For example, an audience of financial officers or engineers will probably have a different disposition than a group of psychologists, yoga students, music teachers, or religious leaders. The first group may be more prone to intellectual activities, while the second group may be more comfortable and used to discussing feelings or spiritual matters.

The purpose is to challenge the natural preferences of the participants, inviting them to step out of their comfort zones in a nonthreatening way and allowing a more holistic involvement. The design will move progressively from the familiar to the less familiar, as trust develops in relationships with the coach and the other participants.

Questions that stimulate exploration of new areas facilitate the integrated journey—for example, moving from thinking to feeling and vice versa. Pauses and general questions, dialogue sessions, journaling, and writing assignments could also be used for this purpose. Guided activities, such as visualization and meditation, as well as tai chi sessions, breathing exercises, or other physical activities are useful resources. Activities that allow creative expression through music, dance, singing, rhythm, painting, and acting are also helpful catalysts for a more holistic involvement of the individual.

Element: Learning and Personality Styles

What is it?

This refers to appreciating and designing learning interventions that accommodate the preferences of all participants in terms of learning and personality styles as well as challenging them so that they are working both within and outside their comfort zones. ARL practitioners also use this element to make participants aware of their own preferences.

When is it applied?

Discovery	Planning	Design and Redesign	Learning Interventions	Evaluation and Debrief

This element is applied during the design process and throughout the Learning Coach's interventions.

How is it applied?

In the design phase, it is important for the coach to anticipate a diverse audience and balance learning activities based on differing learning and personality preferences. Some individuals may prefer intellectual sessions; others may feel more comfortable with hands-on experiences; some may learn best through exchange with others or by reading or writing; and some may be visual, auditory, or kinesthetic learners. Some participants will be introverts and require silence in which to collect their thoughts, while others will be extraverted and need to process their ideas by talking. Learning and participation preferences may also be rooted in cultural habits or values. Scandinavian groups, for example, are more apt to be critical of individuals who are assertive in proclaiming what they know, as this is seen as showing off; however, in American culture such behavior would be taken as active participation.

Interventions that utilize this element are tools that frame an activity by explaining what will be done (the activity and the history and theory behind it), why it will be done (purpose and rationale), how it will be done (steps and processes), and the potential applications and implications of adapting this activity in other situations. Allocating time for silent reflection before a general discussion gives the introverts time to think and also allows the extraverts time to edit their thoughts; then when the discussion begins, everyone is better prepared to listen. There are many tools and techniques that cater to and challenge the various preferences in the room, such as journaling, work in dyads or small groups, hands-on experiences, lectures, and artistic expression sessions.

The ARL practitioner utilizes learning and personality preferences not only to guide interventions but also to expand the perspectives of the learners by sharing with them this aspect of diversity. For this purpose, instruments such as the *Learning-Style Inventory,* the *Emotional Competence Inventory* (ECI), the *Fundamental Interpersonal Relations Orientation–Behavior*™ (FIRO-B®) assessment, and the *Myers-Briggs Type Indicator*® (MBTI®) instrument are valuable resources, as they expand participants' self-awareness and acceptance of differences and of others' learning and personality styles.[29]

Element: Ownership of the Learning

What is it?

This element refers to involving participants in setting both their own learning goals and the expected outcomes of their activities as well as in recommending content and evaluating results.

When is it applied?

Discovery	Planning	Design and Redesign	Learning Interventions	Evaluation and Debrief

This element is important in the discovery (needs assessment) phase, in the planning phase, in the design and organic redesign during the learning intervention, in the Learning Coach's interventions during the session, and in the evaluation and debrief phase.

How is it applied?

The coach promotes ownership in a number of ways: engaging in individual conversations with learners before an activity so as to explore their areas of interest; co-designing sessions; inviting participants to write down their personal learning goals; inviting participants to set norms that promote accountability for their own learning; setting periodic checkpoints for establishing how personal goals are being met; and involving participants in different evaluation processes.

Element: Safe Environment

What is it?

This refers to creating a positive atmosphere that encourages learners to speak up and try out behaviors. Learning environments are safe when individuals can trust one another and people are not judged or ridiculed when they try out new behaviors or express their opinions and perspectives.

When is it applied?

Discovery	Planning	Design and Redesign	Learning Interventions	Evaluation and Debrief

This element is present during the discovery, planning, and design phases and throughout the learning intervention. It is also evident in the evaluation and debrief phase in the Learning Coach's confidential management of the feedback.

How is it applied?

During the needs assessment, coaches guarantee anonymity in their treatment of surveys or interviews. They should be alert to individuals who expect access to information in breach of confidentiality terms. For example, sometimes a manager would like to use a program to obtain information about certain participants without asking them directly. In accepting those expectations, the coach would violate confidentiality and therefore create an unsafe environment.

During the design phase, coaches ensure a safe environment by allocating time for setting norms and being aware of who is attending the session. For example, if outside observers want to attend, their presence may inhibit open discussion.

Finally, during learning interventions and the evaluation and debrief phase, coaches create safe environments through periodically revising agreements, signing confidentiality or nondisclosure documents, conducting activities that explore trust enablers and derailers, running exercises that promote sharing and relationship building, monitoring the climate of the group, and debriefing conflicts collectively in order to extract learnings.

Element: Unfamiliar Environments

What is it?

This refers to exposing learners to unfamiliar situations that can generate reflection and uncover the assumptions they bring to their own mental models.

When is it applied?

Discovery	Planning	Design and Redesign	Learning Interventions	Evaluation and Debrief

The Learning Coach takes this element into account during the planning and designing phases, in deciding on settings, locations, application processes, and selection criteria for participants as well as when grouping criteria and task assignments. Throughout the learning sessions, the coach may use this element as a criterion for stating challenging just-in-time questions or varying the meeting formats in an organic way.

How is it applied?

The coach creates unfamiliar environments by maximizing the diversity (e.g., age, gender, functional, cultural, geographical, ethnic, linguistic, race, religious) within a group, large and small, as well as by conducting activities that require individuals to interact, work, or exchange with others in diverse teams or groups. The choice of the task also helps create an unfamiliar environment, as when individuals are assigned projects or challenges that are outside their habitual domain, knowledge, or experience. The physical environment can also be used for this purpose; for example, the coach may take participants to places that are unknown to them, run a session in an unusual space, or simply remove chairs or tables.

ELEMENTS RELATED TO *WHEN* THE LEARNING COACH ACTS

The ARL coach utilizes the following elements.

Element: Just-in-Time Intervention

What is it?

This refers to the importance of the timeliness of the intervention, introducing concepts, tools, or questions when they are needed.

When is it applied?

Discovery	Planning	Design and Redesign	Learning Interventions	Evaluation and Debrief

This element is important in the discovery phase, when it helps in establishing the current needs of the learners in order to anticipate possible interventions; in the planning phase; during the design and organic redesign; and during interventions, so that the entire process remains flexible and attentive to the evolving dynamics during the session.

How is it applied?

Just-in-time intervention requires the Learning Coach to pay close attention to participants, in order to detect signs of interest, confusion, or anxiety. While it is easy to collect information about the current needs and interests during the discovery and planning phases, this becomes more challenging during the learning sessions. The coach may perceive signs and interpret them as an opportunity for a just-in-time intervention, but it is important to remember that learners must validate the assumption. Therefore, it is valuable to double-check simply by asking and making sure that introduction of a tool or process would be welcome or at least acceptable for everyone. The coach could implement a just-in-time intervention with a pause and a question such as "How are you doing?" as a way of gaining a quick evaluation of the group's level of satisfaction or anxiety. This helps participants take a step away from the action and reflect on whether they may be in difficulty or may need to do something different, which would open the door to the offer of a just-in-time tool.

Element: Sequenced Learning

What is it?

This refers to sequencing modules or meetings over a period of time so that participants can try out what they have learned in their home setting. Then when they return to the learning group, they exchange experiences and lessons and receive feedback and coaching before returning once again to their home setting.

When is it applied?

Discovery	Planning	Design and Redesign	Learning Interventions	Evaluation and Debrief

This element is present during the planning phase, when the Learning Coach organizes the content according to the available time frames. It is also found in the design phase, when the coach allocates time for checking on how participants have been able to transfer and try out what they have learned.

How is it applied?

The coach applies this element during planning by organizing modules separated in time. As for the design, this element is implemented through repetition of topics with different methods or activities that provide opportunities for practice. Other resources include learning partners, peer coaching, general dialogue sessions as follow-up to learning transfer, and tryouts.

THE CENTRAL ELEMENT

The Learning Coach is central to all the other elements.

Element: Learning Coach

What is it?

The Learning Coach is the specialized facilitator who conducts ARL-based learning sessions.

When is it applied?

Discovery	Planning	Design and Redesign	Learning Interventions	Evaluation and Debrief

The Learning Coach is present throughout the entire process, from the assessment of needs to the debrief.

How is it applied?

The Learning Coach plays a number of roles that require different skill sets. Since the initial contact with participants is such a key part of the process, it is important for the Learning Coach to carry out a professional assessment of needs that will inform the planning and design.

The design itself requires attention to detail, rigor, and anticipation during the planning phases but also creativity in developing what needs to be covered while considering the real constraints and possibilities. The organic characteristic of ARL-based interventions requires the Learning Coach to maintain a vigilant attitude and be sensitive to the dynamics and evolution of the learning session in order to make organic redesigns and adjustments.

Another role of the Learning Coach is to offer just-in-time concepts, tools, or input, for which training, attention, and resourcefulness are important ingredients. The Learning Coach also plays certain facilitation roles, such as giving instructions for assignments and summarizing, paraphrasing, or capturing input from participants.

At times, the Learning Coach must play the role of coach, which requires active listening, challenging inquiry, observing and providing feedback, and asking reflective questions.[30]

SUMMING UP

The ARL elements are the common aspects of the shared practice. Each element represents a number of assumptions. And these assumptions, when amplified and elaborated, are connected to the rich and varied theoretical underpinnings of ARL. In the next chapter, we drill down into the assumptions behind the elements explored here.

CHAPTER 11

The Theoretical Foundation of ARL

Part A

Over the years, ARL practitioners have developed their understanding of Action Reflection Learning through the use of tools, frames, experiences, role models, mentors, and conversations with peers, but many also need to know: "What is the theoretical basis that can help explain how ARL works?"

As described earlier, Isabel Rimanoczy and Boris Drizin identified sixteen elements that form the core of the ARL methodology. By analyzing those elements, they were able to identify the assumptions behind them. These assumptions could be traced back to a variety of theories and conceptual frameworks from fields including philosophy; cybernetics; systems theory; broad schools of psychology such as cognitive, behavioral, humanistic, Gestalt, psychoanalysis, and holistic; emotional intelligence; and learning theories such as social learning, experiential learning, transformational learning, and andragogy. In other words, ARL practitioners were putting into practice concepts and theories from diverse social science and learning disciplines.

THE TEN LEARNING PRINCIPLES

As they uncovered these theoretical underpinnings, Rimanoczy and Drizin saw that the assumptions behind certain elements were interconnected. In order to categorize and articulate these interconnections, they identified the existing body of knowledge represented in those assumptions and ten underlying learning principles that describe them best:

- Tacit knowledge

- Reflection

- Repetition and reinforcement

- Uncovering, adapting, and building new mental maps and models

- Social learning

- Facilitated learning

- Relevance

- Integration

- Self-awareness

- Systemic understanding and practice

The first four underlying principles, along with the various ARL elements embodied in each, are discussed in this chapter (Table 4 provides an outline). They emphasize that learning is more than the simple acquisition of new information. Learning is seen as a process in which an individual gains access to tacit knowledge through the activity of reflection; repetition and reinforcement play an important role; and the individual's mental maps and models are uncovered, adapted, and/or built afresh. Each principle synthesizes a distinct group of assumptions, relating to the work of different theorists and brings together a variety of disciplines that explore the processes involved in learning.

TABLE 4. **The First Four Learning Principles and Their Related ARL Elements**

ARL ELEMENT	Tacit Knowledge	Reflection	Repetition and Rein- forcement	New Mental Maps and Models
Guided Reflection				
Feedback				
One-on-One Coaching Support				
Appreciative Approach				
Unfamiliar Environments				
Sequenced Learning				

Learning Principle 1: Tacit Knowledge

Knowledge exists within individuals in implicit, often unseen forms; it is frequently underutilized but can be accessed through guided introspection.

The first learning principle, tacit knowledge, is based on assumptions related to the ARL elements Guided Reflection and One-on-One Coaching Support.

The concept of tacit knowledge was introduced in 1958 by Michael Polanyi in his book *Personal Knowledge*.[31] While explicit knowledge is easy to define, capture, and transfer to different formats, tacit knowledge is difficult to codify and transfer because it is deeply rooted in individual minds. It can also be found within a

**TABLE 5. ARL Elements and Underlying Assumptions
Related to Tacit Knowledge**

ARL ELEMENT	UNDERLYING ASSUMPTIONS
Guided Reflection	■ Reflection helps us connect with our experience and extract the lessons learned from that experience. ■ Reflection sessions need to remain flexible, following the learning needs and dynamics as they unfold, and therefore need to be redesigned frequently to meet an ever-evolving situation that cannot be completely predicted in advance. ■ Activities that foster reflection may help us establish connections and extract meaning of which we would otherwise be unaware.
One-on-One Coaching Support	■ A "talking partner" with a skilled coaching attitude helps us tap into our own resources and answers.

group or a community of practice, in which people act on a knowledge they cannot easily explain or articulate.[32]

Theoretical background

It is easy to recognize the roots of this principle in the work of Socrates, who called it "mayeutics." He suggested that teachers should understand their role as midwives, bringing out of individuals the wisdom that is actually latent in them. This notion is also expressed in the Latin root of the word *education, educere,* meaning "to draw or lead out."

In the realm of education, this principle is seen in the recognition of the learner as an active participant in the learning process. Learners bring a wealth of experiences, ideas, knowledge, and information, which becomes an important component of the learning activity. Contrary to the idea of learners as empty vessels, this perspective values their previous mental models and frameworks, which influence their search for answers and the processing and understanding of new knowledge. From this viewpoint, learners can become active inquirers, and the role of the educator is to provide support in the process of accessing their tacit knowledge.

In the organizational setting, the notion of tacit knowledge has become an important theme in knowledge management.[33] Intellectual capital is increasingly seen as a key organizational asset, even more so than the bricks-and-mortar assets of corporations.[34] As a consequence, organizations have become interested in accessing and capturing this resource hidden in the form of tacit knowledge and distributed across the organization.

Learning Principle 2: Reflection

The ability to thoughtfully reflect on experience is an essential part of the learning process and enables greater meaning and learning to be derived from a given situation.

The second learning principle, reflection, is based on another set of assumptions from the ARL elements Guided Reflection, One-on-One Coaching Support, and Feedback (see Table 6).

Reflection constitutes a basic tenet of ARL practice. We introduced Guided Reflection before as an ARL element, a specific intervention that is implemented through a variety of tools. Guided Reflection, with the emphasis on *Guided,* highlights the fact that someone else is intentionally intervening to foster reflection. Yet reflection by itself is perhaps the most significant principle underlying the ARL practice.

Beginning with the key Greek philosophers Socrates, Plato, and Aristotle, reflection has constituted an essential method for gaining wisdom. In *Theaetetus,* Plato asked: "Why should we not calmly and patiently review our own thoughts, and thoroughly examine and see what these appearances in us really are?"

More recently, a school of thought called "critical reflection" has advanced the power of reflection to question truths, structures, and distribution of power and increase the understanding of

TABLE 6. **ARL Elements and Underlying Assumptions
Related to Reflection**

ARL ELEMENT	UNDERLYING ASSUMPTIONS
Guided Reflection	■ Many individuals tend to spend more time in the arena of action; therefore, an invitation to pause and reflect can create an opportunity to think both before and after acting. ■ To reflect on an action or event is the first step in the learning cycle. ■ To reflect on an action allows the establishment of a subject–object relationship, in which we (the subject) can observe the action (the object), detaching ourselves in order to gain perspective. ■ Reflection helps us connect with our experience and extract the lessons learned. ■ Reflection also helps us imagine scenarios, to anticipate, visualize, and plan.
One-on-One Coaching Support	■ A "talking partner" with a skilled coaching attitude facilitates the assimilation of learning and self-awareness by encouraging more awareness of different perspectives.
Feedback	■ We can learn about ourselves when we reflect on the responses we generate in others. Other people communicating clearly and explicitly about their responses helps greatly with this learning.

self.[35] It is defined as a thinking process that challenges and confronts an individual's own thinking by asking probing questions. For educator Stephen Brookfield, four activities are central to critical reflection:[36]

■ **Assumption analysis:** thinking in a way that challenges our beliefs, values, cultural practices, and social structures in order to assess their impact on our daily behaviors

- **Contextual awareness:** realizing that we create our assumptions socially and personally in specific historical and cultural contexts

- **Imaginative speculation:** thinking in new ways about the same phenomena

- **Reflective skepticism:** questioning what could be presented as universal truths

Critical reflection has also been elevated to the primary objective of adult education in the work of Jack Mezirow: "Perhaps even more central to adult learning than elaborating established meaning schemes is the process of reflecting back on prior learning to determine whether what we have learned is justified under present circumstances. This is a crucial learning process egregiously ignored by learning theorists."[37]

In cognitive psychology, reflection through introspection is seen as an important way of understanding the self.[38] In education, it was John Dewey who first indicated the key role of reflection in the learning process.[39]

Additionally, in the field of education, David Kolb developed a learning cycle of four continuous, cyclically linked phases: concrete experience; reflective observation (critically reflecting on and investigating the experience); abstract conceptualization (developing ideas and hypotheses); and active experimentation (taking action in the world based on our ideas and hypotheses).[40]

Rimanoczy, building on the work of Kolb, developed a change cycle that, by using an event or action as the starting point and reflection as the process, allows an individual to establish connections between the event and its causes in a specific context, an action, and its results.[41] Through the question "What happened?" (feedback), the model explores the individual's own contributions to a specific result (awareness) and then establishes whether there is a need to change anything in that person's behavior. If change is necessary, the individual crafts an actionable and realistic plan, leading to a new action. This action, again, will be observed

FIGURE 5. **The Change Cycle**

5. New Action

4. Plan

1. Feedback

Event/Action
Context

3. Need

2. Awareness

through critical reflection: What happened? Reflection is the process that takes the individual through the cycle, as illustrated in Figure 5. Each of these steps leads to the next, but the cycle could stop at any step, in which case learning is not manifested in behavioral change.

In social research, Kurt Lewin used reflection as a key component of a research method he developed, called "action research."[42] Action research is characterized by continuous cycles of action and reflection—a stage of action based on a possible hypothesis, followed by a stage of reflection in which to evaluate the effects of the action, the validity of the initial hypothesis, and the possible generation of new hypotheses. Action research has become one of the central methods for organizational development.

Other authors in the field of organizational development have created methods to analyze the self and relationships using reflection. Chris Argyris's theory of single- and double-loop learning is based on reflecting on the learning that can be extended beyond a single event to other situations so that the assumptions underpinning these situations can be surfaced and, if necessary, revised.[43]

Donald Schön uses the power of reflection to improve professional practice.[44]

Within all these different conceptual frameworks, reflection constitutes a key factor for learning.

Learning Principle 3: Repetition and Reinforcement

Practice brings mastery, and positive reinforcement increases the assimilation.

The third learning principle, repetition and reinforcement, is based on more assumptions from the ARL element Feedback as well as assumptions from the elements Appreciative Approach and Sequenced Learning (see Table 7).

While many of the other learning principles are found within the constructivist, humanistic, and/or cognitive schools of psychology, this principle is rooted in traditional behavioral psychology.[45] Interestingly, traditional classroom teaching has been heavily influenced by the behaviorist movement, which dominated American psychology from about 1920 to 1970. Behaviorist theory studies empirically observable behaviors as opposed to intangible, more subjective phenomena such as consciousness, feelings, or meanings. Learning depends on interactions with the environment, understanding the individual as, in John Locke's words, a "tabula rasa."

Thus, reinforcements and stimuli play a key role in learning. Edward Thorndike described how changes in behavior (i.e., learning) respond to the Law of Effect: behavior followed by satisfying consequences is more likely to be repeated, while behavior followed by unsatisfying consequences is less likely to be repeated.[46] Internal reinforcement through brain modification was explored by John Watson, an early behavioral psychologist, who in 1902 was one of the first people to obtain a doctorate in psychology in the United States. B. F. Skinner developed the theory of "operant conditioning." He thought that we behave the way we do because a behavior has had certain positive or negative consequences in

TABLE 7. ARL Elements and Underlying Assumptions Related to Repetition and Reinforcement

ARL ELEMENT	UNDERLYING ASSUMPTIONS
Feedback	■ We can learn which aspects of our behavior to keep, emphasize more, or change when we have a better understanding of the impact of our behaviors on others.
Appreciative Approach	■ When we feel accepted (not judged), we are more open to new learning and more able to take risks in public (e.g., being prepared to admit ignorance or try out new behaviors). On the contrary, when we feel judged, we tend to react defensively, retracting or discontinuing new behaviors and reverting to familiar patterns of behavior.
Sequenced Learning	■ The need for new behaviors may be accepted intellectually but should be put into action. • New behaviors may need reinforcement and repetition before they are adopted and assimilated. • When we want to modify our patterns of response, we often need support until the new behaviors become natural.

the past. External reinforcements were further studied by cognitivists David Ausubel and Albert Bandura.[47]

The importance of repetition is highlighted in other intellectual traditions that are very different from behaviorism—for example, in Dewey's discussion of the creation of habits.[48] Dewey himself was influenced by the earlier writings of William James.[49] More recently, Mezirow elaborates on the power of repetition in the establishment of what he calls "habits of mind."[50]

ARL practitioners appear to have incorporated the part of behaviorist thinking that values repetition and reinforcement, acknowledging the importance of supporting active experimentation and offering time and opportunities to try out new behaviors.

They do this through the supportive attitude of the Learning Coach, who ensures that learners feel safe in a trusting and accepting environment and devotes attention to the recognition and appreciation of their achievements.

At the same time, ARL practitioners have let go of other components of behaviorism, such as the neglect of feelings and similarly intangible, more subjective phenomena and the concept of a learner as a tabula rasa—or an empty vessel to be filled with knowledge, passively conditioned by external stimuli and reinforcement.

Learning Principle 4: Uncovering, Adapting, and Building New Mental Maps and Models

The most significant learning occurs when individuals are able to shift the perspective from which they habitually view the world, leading to the capacity for greater understanding (of the world and of others), self-awareness, and intelligent action.

Uncovering, adapting, and building new mental maps and models—the fourth learning principle—is based on assumptions underlying the ARL elements Guided Reflection and Unfamiliar Environments (see Table 8).

Learning principle 4 represents the constructivist paradigm, a reaction against the positivist and postpositivist perspectives that guided the scientific movement until the mid-twentieth century.[51] A paradigm provides a conceptual framework for seeing and making sense of the world and, according to Thomas Kuhn, "stands for the entire constellation of beliefs, values, and techniques, shared by the members of a community."[52]

Paradigms are significant in that they shape how we perceive the world and are reinforced by those around us, in this case by the community of fellow practitioners. According to the positivist paradigm, there is an external, independent reality that science tries to discover, capture, and understand in the form of general laws. It is based on the true–false, right–wrong polarity. In a

TABLE 8. **ARL Elements and Underlying Assumptions Related to Uncovering, Adapting, and Building New Mental Maps and Models**

ARL ELEMENT	UNDERLYING ASSUMPTIONS
Guided Reflection	■ Challenging activities that generate reflection may help us uncover our assumptions.
Unfamiliar Environments	■ Exposure to an unfamiliar environment (situation, task, culture, other individuals) takes us out of our habitual contexts, where we know automatically, and often unconsciously, how to make meaning and how to act. • Habitual behaviors applied to unfamiliar environments may result in unexpected effects. • Unfamiliar environments create powerful experiential learning opportunities. • New situations are opportunities for creative thinking and nontraditional problem solving. • When exposed to unfamiliar environments, we may become aware of our assumptions and habitual behavioral patterns.

positivist view of the world, science is the only valid way to get at truth, to understand the world, and to make valid predictions explaining causal relations between variables. The world and the universe are seen as operated by laws of cause and effect that are discerned by applying the scientific method. Science from a positivist framework is a mechanistic affair.[53]

In the postpositivist paradigm, reality is still out there, waiting to be discovered, but this framework also concedes that it may not be possible to fully grasp reality, given human limitations. The constructivist paradigm, on the contrary, views all of our knowledge as "socially constructed."[54] It does not reflect any external transcendent realities, completely independent of the act of observing them, but is contingent on convention, human perception, and social experience. Thus, the constructivist paradigm replaces the scientific notions of explanation, prediction, and control with the notions of understanding, making meaning, and taking action.[55]

This learning principle is thus based on the constructivist belief that our personal characteristics combined with our particular context and life experience determine a personal map of the world, a particular interpretation and mode of experiencing the world that is mostly subconscious and/or unconscious. We actively interpret the world through the assumptions, language, values, and mental models we develop, influenced by the educational, cultural, family, gender, race, and class contexts in which we live.

As a consequence, our mental maps and models become the interpretative filter through which we interact with others and with the world. As these are so familiar to us and taken for granted, we hardly recognize our view as *a* view, mostly accepting our perception as the true perception of a reality. As Mezirow indicates, it is easier to see how others are different than to realize our own assumptions and meaning structures.[56] Learning to recognize the structure of another person's map allows us to see the world through their eyes and therefore become aware of our own interpretations and meaning schemes. As Henry David Thoreau famously wrote in *Walden,* "Only that day dawns to which we are awake."[57]

Several authors have put forward the importance of uncovering mental maps and models to increase awareness, to produce transformational learning, and/or to augment understanding.[58]

Other educators centered in theories of social action and in feminism highlight the importance of unconscious mental models.[59] They suggest that the main purpose of learning needs to be a critical and self-reflexive process, to uncover and surface these mental models and assumptions in order to expose them to critical scrutiny. Through this challenge, individuals are able to shift the way they interpret the world and take new, more informed and aware action, which, in their perspective, constitutes the real purpose of learning.

This principle, in summary, emphasizes that learning is in essence the process of surfacing and critically scrutinizing the mental models we have created in order to make sense of and act in the world. An important, and at times profound, possible outcome of learning is a different mental model or perspective from which to view the world.

SUMMING UP

In this chapter, we introduced the ten learning principles and then described in detail the assumptions and theoretical foundation of the first four, which are related to the inherent nature of learning.

By highlighting both the process and the outcome of learning, the last principle we described—uncovering, adapting, and building new mental maps and models—provides a bridge into the next chapter, which is concerned with the learning principles that refer to the context and outcomes of learning.

CHAPTER 12

The Theoretical Foundation of ARL

Part B

In chapter 11, we introduced the ten learning principles and described the first four learning principles in detail (see p. 172 for a list of all ten). In this chapter, we examine the last six principles, which as a group tend to address the questions "What is the context in which we learn best?" and "What are the important outcomes of learning?"

THE LAST SIX LEARNING PRINCIPLES

These six underlying principles demonstrate that learning doesn't happen in a vacuum. It happens always in a specific context: with other individuals, in connection with the background of certain challenges or problems, within the frame of specific organizations or institutions to which the individuals belong, and with the support of facilitators who bring a variety of skills and interventions.

Similarly, the learning is connected to outcomes that are related to specific knowledge, contents, development of skills, competencies or mind-sets, self-awareness or attitudes.

The following principles, each of which again synthesizes a distinct group of assumptions, also were found to relate to the work

TABLE 9. **The Last Six Learning Principles and Their Related ARL Elements**

ARL ELEMENT	Social Learning	Facilitated Learning	Relevance	Integration	Self-Awareness	Systemic Understanding and Practice
Appreciative Approach						
Balancing Task and Learning						
Feedback						
Five Dimensions System						
Guided Reflection						
Holistic Involvement of the Individual						

Just-in-Time Intervention	Learning and Personality Styles	Learning Coach	Learning Exchange	Linking	One-on-One Coaching Support	Ownership of the Learning	Safe Environment	Unfamiliar Environments

of theorists from a variety of disciplines who have written about the aspects of context and outcomes involved in learning.

We continue the sequence of the previous chapter by first identifying the elements and assumptions associated with each principle. Then we offer a succinct summary of the principle, followed by further elaboration of the principle in relation to other important theories of learning and development.

Learning Principle 5: Social Learning

Learning emerges through social interaction, and, therefore, individuals learn more with others than by themselves.

The fifth learning principle, social learning, is based on the assumptions related to the ARL elements Learning Exchange and Unfamiliar Environments (see Table 10).

This principle relates to the concept of a socially constructed world.[60] A mutually influencing, dialectical relationship exists between the individual and his or her external reality: we are influenced by the world, and we simultaneously shape the world by our actions and through our interpretations. We inevitably do this within a social context, with its characteristic cultural, economic, ethnic, historical, gender, and race dimensions. Who we are tends to be shaped through interaction with others.

Learning is therefore not an activity that happens in isolation. While the assimilation of learning is personal, a context of social activities always exists to frame and generate learning. Soviet psychologist Lev Vygotsky referred to this as "situated learning," indicating that social interaction plays a key role in the development of cognition.[61] The range of skills that can be developed with guidance or peer collaboration (and also peer competition) exceeds what an individual alone can attain.

Continuing in this line, Jean Lave and Etienne Wenger call this "relational learning" and suggest we change the traditional setup for classroom learning, with its focus on the individual and separation between learners.[62] Social interaction is a critical component of situated learning; learners become involved in what Wenger

**TABLE 10. ARL Elements and Underlying Assumptions
Related to Social Learning**

ARL ELEMENT	UNDERLYING ASSUMPTIONS
Learning Exchange	■ When exchanging perspectives, we surface our own thoughts and opinions and are exposed to the views and questions of others. This may challenge our ways of thinking, provoking revision of assumptions and development of clarity or further exploration. ■ When exchanging perspectives, we learn about the experiences of others, which may enrich our learning.
Unfamiliar Environments	■ Exposure to an unfamiliar environment (e.g., others with different cultures, values, and worldviews) takes us out of our habitual contexts, where we know how to make meaning and act in a taken-for-granted way. Engaging in habitual behaviors with others who are not familiar with us may result in unexpected effects, which can create experiential learning opportunities. ■ Exposure to and interaction with individuals with whom we are not familiar provoke awareness and revision of our assumptions and taken-for-granted behavioral patterns.

terms a "community of practice," which has a particular, shared set of beliefs, history, knowledge, skills, or processes that are common to individuals participating in the community.[63] Lave suggests that situated learning is usually unintentional rather than deliberate.[64] It is noteworthy that the elements of ARL convert the unintentional impact of social learning into an intentional resource that can be planned and incorporated into a learning design.

Canadian author Albert Bandura states: "Learning would be exceedingly laborious, not to mention hazardous, if people had to rely solely on the effects of their own actions to inform them what to do. Fortunately, most human behavior is learned observationally through modeling: From observing others one forms an idea of how new behaviors are performed, and on later occasions this coded information serves as a guide for action."[65] Bandura focuses particularly on the importance of modeling behaviors, which others then adopt. The technique of behavior modeling is coming into wider use in training programs. In recent years, Bandura has used his social learning theory applied to the concept of self-efficacy in a variety of contexts.[66]

Action Learning, the development approach launched by the British physicist Reg Revans in the 1940s, explicitly uses the principle of social learning by grouping individuals into small teams to work together on important real-life organizational problems that need solutions.[67] While Action Learning has spread globally and continues to evolve into many different versions, the practice of individuals banding into small groups to learn together, and from one another, has remained unchanged.[68]

We cite this principle first in this chapter because it emphasizes that learning is a social process involving relationships with others and serves as a complement to the individual process outlined in chapter 11.

Learning Principle 6: Facilitated Learning

A specific role exists for an expert in methods and techniques for teaching and learning who can optimize the learning of both individuals and groups.

As the principle of facilitated learning is at the heart of ARL, it touches on all sixteen ARL elements. However, here we include only the six elements most central to the principle, which are the Learning Coach and the Learning Coach's five main interventions: Feedback, Guided Reflection, Learning Exchange, Linking, and One-on-One Coaching Support (see Table 11).

Within the field of education, there is a long tradition of exploring and discussing the role of an educator. The specific characteristics of the settings, contents to be taught, and contexts, including different traditions and cultures, all have an impact on the type of learner–teacher relationship.

TABLE 11. **ARL Elements and Underlying Assumptions Related to Facilitated Learning**

ARL ELEMENT	UNDERLYING ASSUMPTIONS
Learning Coach	■ Effective learning scenarios require skilled and careful design. ■ Learning sessions must remain flexible, following learning needs and dynamics as they unfold, and therefore should be redesigned frequently to meet an evolving situation that cannot be completely predicted in advance. ■ A skilled coach adds value by carefully and appropriately choosing among a wide range of tools and concepts that can be introduced in both a planned and just-in-time way. ■ One of the roles of a Learning Coach is to create the conditions for best learning.
Feedback	■ When we hear about the impact of our behaviors on others, we can decide which aspects of our behavior to keep, emphasize more, or change. ■ Coaches act as mirrors to help us see other aspects of our own behaviors.
Guided Reflection	■ Many of us, especially in our organizational life, tend naturally to be overly focused on action. Action is often highly valued in organizations. To be able to *reflect* on an action or event is the first step in the learning cycle. ■ Effective learning scenarios require skilled and careful design. ■ A skilled coach fosters insight and learning by introducing activities that help individuals reflect.
Learning Exchange	■ When invited to exchange perspectives, we have an opportunity to surface our own thoughts and opinions and to hear the views and questions of others. ■ Individuals tend to stay in their comfort zone, which deprives them of the exposure to different perspectives that can challenge their assumptions and create learning.

TABLE 11. ARL Elements and Underlying Assumptions Related to Facilitated Learning cont'd

ARL ELEMENT	UNDERLYING ASSUMPTIONS
Linking	• When we become aware of what we are learning, the next step is to consider how the learning could be applied in different situations. • By consciously projecting the learning into other contexts, we are able to convert an experience into a concept or hypothesis that can be tested and adapted to new situations. • By establishing the connection between current learning and other possible applications, we further assimilate the learning, and it becomes easier to remember.
One-on-One Coaching Support	• We learn better when we have coaching support to help us process experiences and extract lessons from them. • A "talking partner" with a skilled coaching attitude facilitates the assimilation of learning and the development of self-awareness.

Directive approaches have been the tradition in hierarchical settings, where power, expertise, and authority reside in the instructor. Instructors, teachers, sports coaches, spiritual masters, or gurus sometimes fall into this category. Some mentors, advisors, counselors, and personal coaches adopt more participative approaches, and while positional power is still an element here, the power may be more balanced or shared than in the traditional approach and the role of power in the relationship is more open to exploration and change.

In educational settings, cognitive psychologists, humanistic-oriented theorists, critical theorists, and learning theorists emphasize different aspects of the role of the teacher or facilitator, but *all* acknowledge the importance of providing support for the learning.[69]

In organizational settings, Edgar Schein, a pioneer in the field of organizational development, introduced the concept of "process consultant," which refers to a person who supports learning for individuals or teams by focusing on the process by which they carry out the task.[70] This facilitator is normally not expected to be a regular member of the team he or she is supporting and for that reason is able to bring a fresh perspective to the problem and to challenge the thinking of team members.

Within Action Learning programs, Revans originally advised against an external facilitator, suggesting that the set members rotate in taking on the role if coordination were needed.[71] As different practitioners experimented with new ways of running Action Learning programs, the role of the "set advisor" developed to include different characteristics.[72] Some approaches to Action Learning include an external coach, with a range of roles—from asking probing questions to challenging team members to take on more involved roles, such as those of facilitator or teacher.[73]

This principle, in common with the learning principle of self-awareness, has the largest number of ARL elements and connected assumptions. ARL is all about learning, and therefore the presence of the learning facilitator, the individual who helps learning occur, is visible throughout the different interventions and throughout all the phases of a learning event, beginning at discovery and ending with the evaluation and debrief.

Learning Principle 7: Relevance

Learning is optimized when the focus of the learning is owned by, relevant to, and important and timely for the individual.

The seventh learning principle brings together assumptions of five ARL elements: Balancing Task and Learning, Five Dimensions System, Just-in-Time Intervention, Linking, and Ownership of the Learning (see Table 12).

The assumptions above help signal a distinction that can be made between educational activities that rely on teachers and

TABLE 12. **ARL Elements and Underlying Assumptions
Related to Relevance**

ARL ELEMENT	UNDERLYING ASSUMPTIONS
Balancing Task and Learning	■ We have an opportunity to learn consciously when attention is given to both what we are doing (the content or task) and how we are performing (the process). ■ When the learning is anchored in and extracted from a real task or a real situation, it becomes more meaningful.
Five Dimensions System	■ It is not enough to develop competencies, knowledge, behaviors, and attitudes in isolation. When learning is focused on a real challenge, it is grounded in reality and becomes more than just an intellectual exercise. This kind of learning has greater meaning and purpose.
Just-in-Time Intervention	■ We learn best when the teaching input is timely and addresses an issue or difficulty with which we are currently grappling.
Linking	■ When we consciously project our learning into other contexts, we are able to convert an actual experience into a concept or hypothesis that can be tested and adapted to new situations. ■ By establishing the connection between a current learning and other possible applications, learning is further assimilated and becomes easier to remember.
Ownership of the Learning	■ When we have an active role in setting the learning agenda, determining the contents we wish to learn, and/or influencing the way these contents are transmitted, our learning is more effective. ■ When we set our learning goals, we are more motivated and involved than those who have no input into their learning agenda.

those that rely on learners themselves. In the former, the emphasis is on the educator as the sole agent of the transmission of knowledge. As Peter Vail indicates, in teaching-based education it is the expert teacher who knows what students have to learn and how they need to learn it.[74] The teacher decides contents and methods. Information and facts are channeled from an "expert" authority to a "novice" subject who is seen as a recipient of that knowledge. The Brazilian educator Paulo Freire called this "the banking approach," in which deposits of knowledge are made into the minds of the students.[75] Patricia Cranton, the Canadian adult education author, notes that such an approach may be the best for certain technical subjects.[76] Furthermore, individuals have their own learning preferences, and a person's personality type or developmental stage may make one approach more appropriate than another.

When the educational activities derive from the learner, the student becomes the actor, or "active inquirer," the term used when discussing principle 1, tacit knowledge. In this approach, it is the active exploration of one's experiences and thoughts, more than the input of the instructor, that generates the learning. This has been called experiential learning by the American educators John Dewey, Eduard Lindeman, and David Kolb.[77] Other authors have referred to this approach—by which individuals use their current reality as the most important arena for learning—as situated learning and Action Learning.[78] (These are outlined in this chapter in the section on principle 5, social learning, and in chapter 11.) The educational traditions in which individuals play an important role in identifying their own learning needs have been referred to as "learner-centered" approaches. These traditions were described extensively by Malcolm Knowles as "andragogy."[79] Knowles was a pioneer in redefining adult learning as different from pedagogy and introducing four important themes: self-directed learning, use of experience, readiness to learn, and performance-centered orientation to learning.

This learning principle, relevance, is at the heart of andragogy and other learner-centered approaches to education such as inquiry learning.[80] Other significant educationalists such as Freire, in his 1970 work on popular education, *Pedagogy of the Oppressed,* also refer to the importance of relevance. Kurt Lewin, founder of Action Research, highlights the importance of using real, current events to extract learning, so that it is meaningful and applicable to other contexts.[81]

More recently, Lave refers to this principle by stating the importance of presenting the information in a real context, that is, in the setting and for the application that relates to that knowledge.[82] This principle has also been the core of work-based learning, a concept developed by Joseph Raelin and applied to management development, with the manager's real work challenges and/or projects becoming the focus of the learning.[83]

In summary, this principle has been the foundation of many significant, innovative approaches to education and management development that have sought to break away from the restrictions and hierarchical power relationships of traditional classroom, teacher-centered approaches to learning.

Learning Principle 8: Integration

People are a combination of mind, body, spirit, feelings, and emotions, and they respond best when all aspects of their being are considered, engaged, and valued.

This learning principle brings together assumptions contained in two ARL elements: Appreciative Approach and Holistic Involvement of the Individual (see Table 13).

This principle is deeply rooted in humanistic psychology. During the first half of the twentieth century, American psychology was dominated by two schools of thought: behaviorism and psychoanalysis. They didn't focus on values or try to comprehend people in the terms the individuals themselves used. In reaction to this, in 1957 Abraham Maslow and Clark Moustakas initiated

TABLE 13. **ARL Elements and Underlying Assumptions Related to Integration**

ARL ELEMENT	UNDERLYING ASSUMPTIONS
Appreciative Approach	▪ When we feel accepted (not judged), we are more open to new learning and to taking risks in public (such as admitting ignorance or trying out new behaviors).
Holistic Involvement of the Individual	▪ When we feel accepted in all our human dimensions, our defensiveness diminishes and we often express ourselves more fully. ▪ In organizations, individuals tend to be pushed into living fragmented lives, in which their cognitive functioning is prioritized and rewarded, leaving out the emotional and spiritual dimensions. Fragmented or divided lives do not allow for a full expression of the self. ▪ When we are able to express ourselves by integrating our emotions and spiritual aspirations, we have more fulfilling experiences and relate to others in an expansive, energizing, and positive way. ▪ In organizations, individuals typically don't have many opportunities to express the full range of their being and welcome those opportunities when they occur. ▪ We are more open to learning when we can be ourselves in a fuller, integrated way.

forums and invited psychologists who were interested in considering a more humanistic vision, thereby launching a new movement. They discussed themes such as self-actualization, health, creativity, intrinsic nature, being, becoming, individuality, and meaning—which they considered key for a different approach to psychology. A few years later, the American Association for Humanistic Psychology was founded, listing as members Gordon Allport, Charlotte Buhler, Abraham Maslow, Rollo May, and Carl Rogers, among others. This movement aimed at a fuller concept of what it means to be human. It reflected thoughts expressed long ago by other civilizations such as those of the Hebrews, the Greeks, and the Renaissance Europeans.

Rogers used the inspiration of the humanistic approach to develop a therapeutic model called "person-centered therapy."[84] The power of this approach is based on the role of the therapist, who offers empathetic understanding, appreciation, and a supportive attitude. Humanistic psychology has a hopeful, constructive view of human beings and of their substantial capacity for self-determination. As a consequence, it promotes choice, creativity, interaction of the body, mind, and spirit, and the capacity to become more aware, free, and responsible.

Humanistic psychology suggests that all learning is emotionally grounded and that our mental models are not just cognitive constructs but are also attached to deep levels of identity and feelings. Therefore, any engagement with learning at a more than superficial level is also an engagement with emotion. Daniel Goleman has developed the concept of emotional intelligence, acknowledging the importance of emotions in our thinking and acting.[85]

More recently, other humanistic-based theories have attempted to integrate spiritual and different cultural perspectives in order to more fully understand the range of human experience. American philosopher and prolific writer Ken Wilber has developed an integral theory of consciousness that draws on disciplines such as psychology, sociology, philosophy, mysticism, postmodernism, empirical science, Buddhism, and systems theory.[86] Elizabeth Tisdell incorporates spirituality into the learning process, to allow participants a full expression of themselves.[87]

David Cooperrider and Diana Whitney developed Appreciative Inquiry, another approach broadly rooted in humanistic psychology.[88] Grounded in the theory of social constructionism (a constructivist paradigm), this approach suggests that human systems, such as organizations, are constructions of the imagination and that, therefore, changing the way we habitually imagine and socially construct organizations together leads to changes in organizational functioning.[89]

According to Cooperrider and Whitney, Appreciative Inquiry seeks to build a constructive union between "a whole people and the massive entirety of what people talk about as past and present capacities: achievements, assets, unexplored potentials, innovations, strengths, elevated thoughts, opportunities, benchmarks, high point moments, lived values, traditions, strategic competencies, stories, expressions of wisdom, insights into the deeper corporate spirit or soul—and visions of valued and possible futures."[90]

This approach points out that the manner in which we conduct any inquiry affects the reality that is evoked. If we ask questions aimed at uncovering what is working well, we will shape a reality that is more positive and more open to learning and change. Appreciative Inquiry uses the strengths and successes of individuals and organizations to enhance self-esteem, encourage action, and demonstrate that people are capable of valuable achievements.

Integration as described above is strongly related to the following ARL principle, self-awareness, which involves an awareness of all dimensions of the self, not just the cognitive dimension.

Learning Principle 9: Self-Awareness

Building self-awareness through helping people understand the relationship between what they feel and think, how they act, and their impact on others is a crucial step to greater personal and professional competence.

The ninth learning principle brings together assumptions of eight different ARL elements: Appreciative Approach, Feedback, Guided Reflection, Holistic Involvement of the Individual, Learning and Personality Styles, One-on-One Coaching Support, Safe Environment, and Unfamiliar Environments (see Table 14).

"Know thyself" was the ancient Greek aphorism inscribed in golden letters at the entrance to the Temple of Apollo at Delphi. John Locke's chapter "On Identity and Diversity," in his *An Essay*

Concerning Human Understanding (1689), is one of the first modern conceptualizations of "consciousness," a term close to "self-awareness." In Locke's writing, consciousness meant recognizing oneself, and only after doing so could any moral responsibility be attributed to the subject. According to Locke, personal identity (the self) depends on consciousness, not on substance or the soul.

Since Locke, many writers have stressed the significance of self-awareness. Within the domain of behavioral sciences, William James described the role of introspection in increasing self-awareness.[91] Sigmund Freud and later authors influenced by his writings (Anna Freud, Carl Jung, Wilhelm Reich, Alfred Adler, Melanie Klein, D. W. Winnicott, and Jacques Lacan, to name a few) extensively examined the importance of exploring emotions, feelings, and thoughts to uncover the unconscious reasons for our reactions and behaviors.[92] Also, in the Third Force, an alternative name for humanistic psychology, self-awareness is seen as a way of expanding our understanding of ourselves and improving our relationships with others.

Jung's work defining psychological types was the foundation for the instrument developed by Katharine Briggs and Isabel Myers, the *Myers-Briggs Type Indicator®* (MBTI®) instrument, which assesses behavioral preferences and personality characteristics.[93] The MBTI inventory is one of the most common psychological instruments used to increase self-awareness.

In the field of management literature, Peter Senge introduced "self mastery" as one of the five basic disciplines necessary for building "learning organizations."[94] Goleman described a distinct perspective on intelligence in which an intellectually based intelligence, or IQ, is replaced by a much broader concept of intelligence involving the ability to understand one's own and others' emotions.[95] In this perspective, self-awareness plays a key role in personal competence and self-management.

In the educational field, Jack Mezirow repeatedly elaborated on the importance of uncovering one's assumptions as the beginning step on a road leading to increased self-awareness.[96] As a

TABLE 14. **ARL Elements and Underlying Assumptions Related to Self-Awareness**

ARL ELEMENT	UNDERLYING ASSUMPTIONS
Appreciative Approach	■ When we feel accepted (not judged), we are more open to new learning and to taking risks in public (such as reflecting on self or admitting difficulties)
Feedback	■ We have an opportunity to develop greater self-understanding by exploring how we contribute to the responses we evoke.
Guided Reflection	■ Reflecting on our own contributions to a problem or situation can deepen our self-awareness. ■ Reflecting on an action allows us to establish a subject–object relationship, in which we (the subject) can observe the action (the object), detaching ourselves in order to gain perspective. ■ Reflection may help uncover our assumptions. ■ Reflection helps us connect with our experience and extract lessons learned.
Holistic Involvement of the Individual	■ Fragmented or divided lives do not allow for full expression of the self. ■ When we are able to express ourselves, integrating our emotions and our spiritual aspirations, we have more fulfilling experiences and relate to others in an expansive, energizing, and positive way. ■ We are more open to learning when we can be ourselves in a fuller, integrated way.
Learning and Personality Styles	■ Finding out more about learning and personality style differences helps us understand both ourselves and the ways in which people are different.
One-on-One Coaching Support	■ A "talking partner" with a skilled coaching attitude facilitates the assimilation of learning and the development of greater self-awareness.

**TABLE 14. ARL Elements and Underlying Assumptions
Related to Self-Awareness** cont'd

ARL ELEMENT	UNDERLYING ASSUMPTIONS
Safe Environment	▪ When we know and agree with the "rules of the game," we feel more confident, trust levels increase, and we may feel more comfortable with searching for personal insightsselves in a fuller, integrated way.
Unfamiliar Environments	▪ When exposed to unfamiliar environments, we may become more aware of assumptions and behavioral patterns we take for granted. Apprehending our own assumptions, ways of making meaning, and typical behavioral patterns leads to increased self-awareness as well as a fuller understanding and appreciation of the behaviors and differences of others.

result, he argued, individuals may experience transformational learning. Many other educational authors have referred to the importance of uncovering assumptions to increase both self-awareness and awareness of the social, political, and cultural environments to which the self is indissolubly connected.[97]

Self-awareness is to us one of the most important principles underlying the ARL learning methodology, as it connects to the highest number of ARL elements with assumptions. It is also a key component of an effective Learning Coach, as explained in chapter 13.

Learning Principle 10: Systemic Understanding and Practice

We live in a complex, interconnected, co-created world, and in order to better understand and tackle individual and organizational issues, we have to take into account the different systems and contexts that mutually influence one another.

The tenth learning principle brings together the assumptions behind two ARL elements: Five Dimensions System and Linking (see Table 15).

This principle has its roots in systems theory. In order to understand it, a brief account of the development of systems thinking in the twentieth century will be useful.

The Austrian biologist Ludwig von Bertalanffy proposed system theory in the 1940s.[98] Reacting to the dominant reductionist approach in science, Bertalanffy posited that all elements of any living system were connected, creating webs of relationships. The properties of the whole were different from the sum of the components, and the components influenced both one another and the whole. Instead of thinking of an entity in terms of the characteristics and functioning of its separate parts—for example, the organs or cells of the human body—system theory considers how they are interrelated and how they function to create a whole. Systems thinking deals with wholes rather than parts and considers relationships and processes rather than separate entities.[99]

At around the same time, the concept of interrelated parts was also present in the field of cybernetics. Cybernetics is the study of communication and control, typically involving regulatory feedback in living organisms, machines, and organizations. Elements are seen as related to one another through transfer of information and circular relations, called "feedback." A diverse group of researchers—American mathematician Norbert Wiener, British psychiatrist William Ross Ashby, Hungarian mathematician John von Neumann, and Austrian physicist and philosopher Heinz von Foerster—gathered in the 1940s and 1950s and, in their discussions, founded the field of cybernetics.

The American cultural anthropologist Margaret Mead and her husband, Gregory Bateson, also participated in these meetings and contributed significantly to the development of the field. Bateson's work has been extended further through the application of system theory to family therapy and neuro-linguistic programming. Mead

TABLE 15. ARL Elements and Underlying Assumptions Related to Systemic Understanding and Practice

ARL ELEMENT	UNDERLYING ASSUMPTIONS
Five Dimensions Systems	■ When personal attitudes are not sufficiently considered, learning remains a technical exercise that may lack the behavioral support and/or motivation required. ■ When skills and competencies are not sufficiently considered, we as learners may have difficulty translating our best intentions into actions. ■ When the learning is not transferred to the team(s) with which we as learners interact, we may have more difficulty implementing and maintaining new behaviors, as the system acts to pull us back into known patterns and habitual interactions. ■ When the larger organizational system is not consistent with the new behaviors we want to adopt (i.e., it does not support, reward, acknowledge, incorporate, or accommodate the behaviors), it becomes very difficult for us to integrate and sustain these behaviors. ■ Learning happens best when it is anchored in real, current challenges or problems with which learners are engaged.
Linking	■ Connecting what is being experienced or learned with other contexts, outside the here and now, allows us to expand our perspectives and understandings and discover new relations and interconnectedness.

used the concepts of positive and negative feedback in her work as a social scientist.

In the behavioral sciences, a similar way of thinking had already begun to emerge through the Gestalt psychology movement in the first half of the twentieth century, spearheaded by German researchers Max Wertheimer, Kurt Koffka, Kurt Lewin, and Wolfgang Köhler, who in 1929 published his book *Gestalt Psychology*. Wertheimer applied Gestalt theory to problem solving and posited that the separate parts of a problem should not be studied in isolation but should instead be seen as a whole. Lewin, in turn, developed his field theory based on Gestalt principles, which indicated that behavior is determined by the totality of an individual's situation as opposed to a single cause-and-effect relationship. In his theory, a field is defined as "the totality of coexisting facts which are conceived of as mutually interdependent," which again stresses connectivity and interrelatedness as key to comprehension.[100]

More recently, systemic thinking has been applied in numerous fields, such as sociology; political science and social action; business, management, and organizational theory; psychotherapy; economics; and ecology.[101] Developmental psychologists and behavioral researchers (e.g., Robert Kegan, William Torbert, Ken Wilber) consider a systems perspective in their theories. Sustainability theories are rooted in the interrelatedness of economy, ecology, and social equity and underscore the importance of acknowledging the interrelatedness of all things.[102]

Probably closest to the field of learning, Senge's *The Fifth Discipline* (1990) introduced the concept of systems thinking as one of the five basic disciplines that would allow an organization to learn. He saw the ability of individuals and teams to expand thinking in order to include different perspectives and move beyond the immediate stimulus–response connections as a key factor in surviving in a complex and fast-changing world.

It is no accident that systemic understanding and practice is the last of the ten key learning principles to be presented. By stating that learning always happens in a systemic context, and that the different levels of any context (e.g., individual, team, organizational, social/political, and ecological) are always interrelated, this principle integrates and connects the other nine principles.

SUMMING UP

Going back to the original question posed at the beginning of chapter 11—"What is the theoretical basis that can help explain how ARL works?"—these chapters have taken you on another journey. Starting with the sixteen ARL elements used by ARL practitioners, as identified in primary research, Rimanoczy and Drizin were able to clarify and articulate the underlying assumptions behind each element. It was then possible to recognize the related theoretical foundations, which in turn were derived from a diversity of disciplines, as we have seen in this and the previous chapter.

It is particularly interesting that the practitioners of ARL have spontaneously brought together concepts and perspectives from divergent paradigms, which many times are so different that they apparently contradict and exclude one another. The practice of ARL has hereby become a rich and unusual synthesis. While conceptual frameworks and theoretical constructs offer an in-depth interpretation of some parts of reality—of learning, social interactions, human behavior, change, and so on—skilled ARL practitioners use all the resources they consider helpful, creatively combining them to meet the needs of different situations and to align with their own personal style and values as Learning Coaches.

Whether their interventions fit neatly into one or another school of thought seems to be no longer important. With a sense of conceptual freedom, ARL practitioners make their decisions, both planned in advance and moment to moment as their work unfolds, based on their reflections on the results of their practice so that they can do it better next time. Independent of the mandates of theories, ARL practitioners engage in the reality of the situations in which they find themselves working, with the full range of intellectual, emotional, and behavioral resources at hand and with the overall aim of generating the greatest learning for participants. Other chapters in this book have illustrated the potential variety of the situations in which ARL can be applied.

What does it take to be able to act with that level of freedom and professional concern at the same time? What does it take to be aware of the changing patterns and interrelationships among individual, group, and organizational learning needs and dynamics and integrate them into an effective learning intervention, consistent with the individual style of the Learning Coach? In the next chapter, we explore the key roles of the Learning Coach and the skills and mind-sets that shape them.

CHAPTER 13
▼

The Learning Coach

Let's step back for a moment and review where we have been on this journey. In part 1, you had a brief introduction into the world of adult learning and Action Reflection Learning. In parts 2 and 3, we plunged into the reality of the practice. You were able to observe different settings in which learning happened and read about the learning interventions, which represent only a small aspect of ARL—like the visible part of an iceberg (see Figure 6).

In parts 2 and 3, in the closest approximation to a just-in-time intervention we could devise, you found highlighted ARL elements—lying just under the surface—demonstrated in a specific intervention. This arrangement gave you a conceptual framework, guided you through the complexities of the practice, and showed the logic supporting the specific interventions. You were able to follow the thinking and hesitations of a Learning Coach engaged in ARL-based practice.

In part 4, we focused in greater depth on the assumptions that underlie the ARL elements and those interventions. Then we connected the ARL assumptions with the theoretical foundations to explain the power of those assumptions in action.

FIGURE 6. **Interventions, Elements, Assumptions, and Theoretical Foundations of ARL**

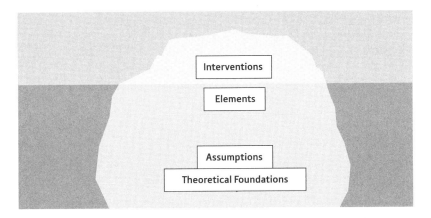

In this chapter, we explore the other components that lie under the surface of the Learning Coach's interventions. We describe and explain the roles, knowledge, competencies, and profile required for a coach working with the ARL methodology. But before we start, it seems appropriate to define what we mean by *Learning Coach.*

THE LEARNING COACH

Twenty years ago, we all knew what a coach was: a person in the athletic sports arena who knew how to boost the performance of individuals or teams. But in the late 1980s, the title began to be used to identify other types of support personnel. Image consultants, financial advisors, public-speaking trainers, strategy and business consultants all started to call themselves *coaches.* The term continued to expand and include other areas of individual and organizational development, adopting niche distinctions such as life coaches, career coaches, transition coaches, executive coaches, business coaches, and even a new leadership profile, the "leader-coach."

Within that wide coaching landscape, what exactly is a Learning Coach?[103] The Learning Coach operates simultaneously in the five dimensions of ARL, which we covered in chapter 10 (see pp. 157–159):

- The business dimension

- The organizational dimension

- The professional dimension

- The personal dimension

- The team dimension

While the Learning Coach wears different hats (using process consulting skills, facilitation skills, and teaching or reflecting skills), the common denominator is the ultimate aim of creating learning. The main function and objective of the Learning Coach in the ARL intervention is to create a helping relationship that supports individuals in achieving their learning objectives. This involves unlocking participants' potential; providing options to maximize their performance; guiding them toward increased competence, commitment, and confidence; and providing a learning arena for sustained cognitive, emotional, and behavioral changes.

We now will explore what it takes to do so.

RESOURCES OF THE LEARNING COACH

We use the term *resources* to refer to the array of options a Learning Coach has for making interventions and contributions and for supporting the learning process.

Personality and Preferences

Resources are shaped by the personality characteristics and preferences that distinguish the personal style of the Learning Coach. These preferences are the result of innate tendencies conditioned by family background and cultural, social, economic, gender, ethnic, and life experiences.

Knowledge and Expertise

Resources are also conditioned by knowledge and expertise. We distinguish between knowledge and expertise based on British psychologist John Heron's model of a hierarchy of knowledge.[104] The hierarchy comprises four levels:

- **Experiential knowing**, the bottom level, is what we know through attunement with the present situation but of which we are not necessarily aware.

- **Presentational knowing**, the next level up, refers to knowledge we are able to express through artistic practice or in other symbolic ways—for example, when we express feelings through dance, use metaphors, and so on.

- **Propositional knowing**, the next level, represents what we are able to describe and explain in clear statements. An example could be a lecture on how to prepare a financial report or how to coach.

- **Practical knowing**, the top level of Heron's model, refers to the knowledge put into action. We not only are able to describe something but are actually able to do it with proficiency. We are enacting our knowledge.

The Learning Coach draws on resources using only the top two levels of knowledge: the propositional level, which we call "knowledge," and the practical level, which we call "expertise."

All of us, Learning Coaches included, acquire knowledge and expertise through external inputs (other individuals, lectures, reading) and through experiences. There is a two-way, mutually influencing relationship between knowledge and experience. Debriefing helps Learning Coaches learn from their experiences and build up their knowledge base. At the same time, their knowledge informs their experiences.

To take a very simple example, a Learning Coach may experience a difficult conversation with a colleague. She reflects on it, reaches a conclusion about what she could or should have done, and tries to understand why the other person reacted the way he did. She happens to read an article about difficult conversations and compares the new perspectives with her experience. She recognizes some similar traits, confirms some of the lessons she extracted, challenges some of them in view of the new input, and gains some new perspectives by realizing that she herself contributed significantly to the problem. As a result, she may decide to approach her colleague again and try to resolve the argument, enriched with her new perspective.

Not all experience becomes expertise. But when the knowledge–experience dialectic repeats often enough, expertise can develop. At that point the individual is able not only to perform a task but also to combine more creatively what he or she knows and apply it to specific situations. To return to our example, when the Learning Coach approaches her colleague to solve the conflict and try out what she's learned, she may realize the new approach works fine and keep it in mind when handling a difficult conversation in the future. After some time, she may be able to avoid getting into difficult conversations with others because she is alert to how she may be contributing to the problem, and that alone makes her change her approach.

In summary, the individual builds up a reservoir of resources that originates in his or her knowledge and expertise and is shaped by personality characteristics and preferences. All of these factors affect the assumptions underlying the Learning Coach's visible interventions, as shown in Figure 7.

Values and Emotional Intelligence

Our values—which are shaped by as well as shape our personality preferences and experience—have an equal impact on our assumptions. The background of emotional intelligence, which provides balance and a permanent quest for deepening a Learning Coach's

FIGURE 7. **Dynamics Affecting Resources**

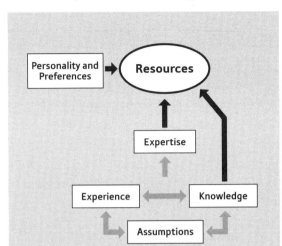

FIGURE 8. **Values and the Background of Emotional Intelligence**

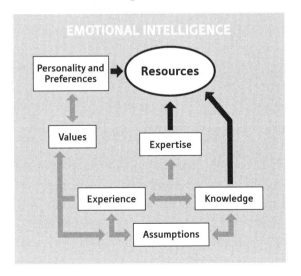

self-awareness, is another addition to this complex map (see Figure 8). By understanding the self better, the Learning Coach is able to recognize his or her strengths and limitations, and this recognition serves as an additional resource and tends to result in more insightful interventions.[105]

FIGURE 9. **The Complete Intervention Picture**

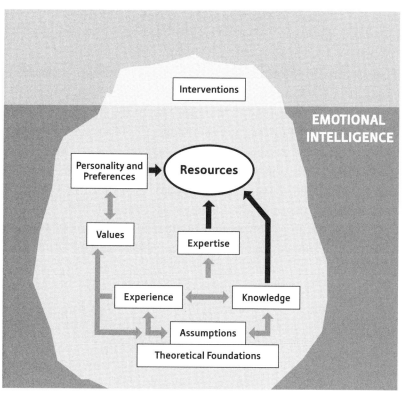

THE COMPLETE PICTURE

Looking back at Figure 6, which shows an iceberg made up of visible interventions and the invisible assumptions beneath the surface, we can now see the other components that underlie the visible interventions of a Learning Coach. Knowledge and experience create expertise, but there is also a systemic interconnectedness between them, the personality characteristics and preferences, the values, and the assumptions we as Learning Coaches make. All these components feed into one another and are supported and influenced by our emotional intelligence (see Figure 9).

USING THE RESOURCES: AN ARL COACH IN ACTION

In the stories we have shared so far, you have seen Learning Coaches involving themselves in a variety of interventions. At times, they acted as facilitators; at other times, they were coaches or instructors. As facilitators, they focused both on the process and on progress with the task. As coaches or instructors, they were sensitive to learning styles and personality preferences; they challenged the assumptions or comfort zones of the learners. They constantly used questions and fostered reflection in a variety of ways. They introduced just-in-time concepts and tools. At times, they "held the space" by providing a safety net so that individuals and teams could take risks as they tried new ways of handling uncertainty.

Importantly, they showed their own openness to their ongoing learning. They acted from the belief that individuals can change and that they have within themselves the answers to their own dilemmas. Learning Coaches also looked for ways of extending the lessons from one situation to others by asking, "So how does what we've just learned relate to other parts of your work and life?"

These are just some of the interventions a Learning Coach makes. The variety and broad spectrum of a Learning Coach's interventions and contributions are understandable only when we think of the comprehensive theoretical framework of learning principles behind the practice we presented in the previous chapters. If those ten principles support learning, it should be no surprise that the interventions themselves cover such a broad area.

In order to help shed some light on what may seem an impossible-to-master job, we now take a closer look at how the Learning Coach's skills, knowledge, mind-sets, and attitudes come into play during the interventions.

SKILLS, KNOWLEDGE, MIND-SETS, AND ATTITUDES OF AN ARL COACH

As indicated by the stories in earlier chapters, the Learning Coach wears different hats and plays a variety of roles. In chapter 10, we presented the sixteen ARL elements and discussed how each was used in the different phases of a learning process: discovery, planning, design and redesign, learning interventions, and evaluation and debrief.

We will now use the same sequence to describe the skills, knowledge, mind-sets, and attitudes that are required for a Learning Coach in each of those phases.

Discovery

Discovery	Planning	Design and Redesign	Learning Interventions	Evaluation and Debrief

For the Learning Coach, this is an appropriate juncture for exploring the purpose of the learning—what is required and why it is necessary. This requires an understanding of the learners' perspectives on what they need to learn as well as the viewpoints of other stakeholders within the organization. This is also the time to explore issues of power, to uncover whose interests and agendas are at play as well as whose voices are and should be included. It is important to get everyone's input in this phase. At this time, the Learning Coach must also do the following:

- Explore the consistency between the organization's espoused values and behaviors and its actual, practiced values and behaviors, as well as the organizational setting in which those values and behaviors exist

- Examine stakeholders' expectations and determine how they match the resources available, time required, and commitment needed

- Extract lessons from past experiences regarding what should be repeated and what should be avoided

- Identify those assumptions that need to be tested and confirmed if the learning aspirations (goals and outcomes) are to be realized

Required Skills/Knowledge:

- Meeting, planning, and management skills

- Inquiry skills including questioning techniques

- Understanding of power dynamics and the characteristics of change processes within the organizational setting and within the individual

- Contracting skills—it is critical that coaches establish a clear understanding with individuals and groups about what they will and will not do as a coach; learners, especially when under stress, may have unrealistic and unmet expectations of them

- Ability to negotiate realistic learning interventions that adhere to ARL principles

- Ability to establish a focus for learning at multiple levels

- Understanding of the context—for example, the type of organizational culture and current challenges the group or organization is facing, not only internally, but also in relation to the community, market, and environment

Required Mind-sets/Attitudes:

- Positive, can-do attitude

- Appreciative approach that recognizes and builds on strengths and past successes

- Systems perspective that encompasses the interests and needs of a variety of stakeholders

- Balance of flexibility and firmness
- Results orientation

Planning

Discovery	Planning	Design and Redesign	Learning Interventions	Evaluation and Debrief

In the planning phase, the Learning Coach analyzes the information collected during the discovery phase and uses it to develop a proposal replete with a list of outcomes, a suggested time frame, and the sequence of the learning interventions. The coach is attentive to the size of the learning group, the location of the meeting, and the overall contents to be covered. This is also the time when the coach makes recommendations and decisions about pedagogical methodologies and resources.

Required Skills/Knowledge:

- Expertise in planning the particular type of intervention (conference, lecture, workshop, or longer program, or an intervention for an individual or group)

- Knowledge of ARL principles and elements that can inform the coach about areas requiring attention when crafting the plan

- Checklists that guide and support program planning

Required Mind-sets/Attitudes:

- Rigor and attention to detail
- Outside-the-box thinking that allows for more creative combinations of resources
- Ability to anticipate potential pitfalls and obstacles

Design and Redesign

Discovery	Planning	Design and Redesign	Learning Interventions	Evaluation and Debrief

During the design of a learning intervention, the Learning Coach takes the draft outline prepared during the planning phase to the next level of detail, mapping out individual sessions with specific contents. The activities, time frames, and required materials and other resources are clearly defined. Redesign work is done periodically based on feedback from participants and other stakeholders during the delivery phase. Skills, knowledge, mind-sets, and attitudes that are valuable in the planning phase are needed here as well, with some additions.

Required Skills/Knowledge:

- Expertise in planning the particular type of intervention (conference, lecture, workshop, or longer program, or an intervention for an individual or a group)

- Knowledge of ARL principles and elements that can inform the coach about areas requiring attention when crafting the plan

- Checklists that guide and support program planning

- Tool kit including learning activities, learning dynamics, and teaching techniques

Required Mind-sets/Attitudes:

- Rigor and attention to detail

- Out-of-the-box thinking that allows for more creative combinations of resources

- Ability to anticipate potential pitfalls and obstacles

- Flexibility—a map is never exactly the same as the terrain of real-life situations

- Ability to balance flexibility with firmness, judging when to change course and when to follow the design in hand

- Ability to handle the unexpected without panic

Learning Interventions

Discovery	Planning	Design and Redesign	Learning Interventions	Evaluation and Debrief

Once the initial design has been approved and participants are present, the time for on-site learning interventions begins.

As we have shown in previous chapters, the complexity and variety of the learning theories that constitute the ARL methodology result in a combination of different learning interventions. These interventions fall into three groups:

- Facilitation

- Coaching

- Teaching

Each group's ultimate focus is on learning. The act of facilitation ensures the extraction of learning, and the same happens with the coaching and teaching interventions. The Learning Coach is distinguished by precisely the combination of the three roles, with learning as the overarching goal (see Figure 10).

We have categorized the Learning Coach's interventions into these three related areas so that we can better describe the knowledge, skills, and mind-sets the coach needs to master. Once the intervention is under way, these roles become interconnected, as the various knowledge bases, skill sets, and mental models are required at different phases of any learning intervention.

FIGURE 10. **Roles of the Learning Coach**

We believe that in order to avoid confusion, the Learning Coach should make the change of roles explicit when he or she is going from facilitator to teacher or to coach. For example, after the Learning Coach introduces a new concept or a tool (teaching role), a participant may ask a question about how such a tool could be applied in his current challenge. The Learning Coach can reply from within the teaching role or may see this as the opportunity for a coaching intervention. After indicating a change in role, instead of answering the question the coach could ask the group to take a moment and reflect on how to adapt the tool to the participant's challenge.

Although the interventions are grouped according to their focus on facilitation, teaching, or coaching, they are all learning interventions. The Learning Coach's ultimate responsibility is to extract the most learning from each activity.

Facilitation

In the facilitation role, Learning Coaches must master tools and techniques well known to experienced facilitators. As in previous phases, an overall systemic perspective is most valuable.

Required Skills/Knowledge:

- Ability to foster and ensure dialogue and democratic participation

- Competence in facilitation of divergent thinking sessions (e.g., brainstorming, problem analysis) and convergent processes (e.g., decision making, problem solving, time management)

- Ability to create a safe, relaxed, trusting environment

- Attention to improving work on the task

- Ability to clearly communicate instructions

- Observation and listening skills

- Ability to manage tension and disruptive behaviors

- Understanding of group dynamics and human interaction

- Understanding of how power is exercised within a group setting

- Understanding of the cultural background of participants and/or the organization in which the learning takes place

Required Mind-sets/Attitudes:

- Sensitivity to diversity and to individuals' feelings

- Self-awareness

- Patience

- Focus on balance of task accomplishment with process and learning

- Openness to feedback

- Flexibility to adapt and adjust to emerging needs

- Appreciative approach combined with a positive, can-do attitude to serve as a role model and positive mirror for participants

Coaching

In the coaching role, many of the techniques familiar to executive coaches are applicable to both individual and collective ARL-based learning interventions. One key competency is inquiry (the use of questions), which may be used for a variety of purposes: to probe, challenge, explore, clarify, generate reflection, expand the thinking, and link to other contexts. The coach's proficiency in asking good questions will have a great impact on the results achieved.

Coaches are frequently puzzled or amazed by the lack of responsiveness some participants demonstrate in learning interventions. For example, participants may find it difficult to engage in reflective practices that invite them to consider alternate perspectives. Other participants expect the Learning Coach to tell them what to learn and feel uncomfortable assuming responsibility for their own learning. Robert Kegan's conceptual framework describes the different ways in which individuals make meaning and explains that we are all in different developmental stages.[106] This notion helps Learning Coaches tailor interventions to individual needs.

Required Skills/Knowledge:

- Inquiry (as described above)
- Use of both wording and a confident personal tone to create a safe, trusting, appreciative, energizing, nonjudgmental environment
- Ability to run guided reflection and visualization activities
- Understanding of personality types and adult development stages
- Understanding of the psychology of human interactions, including the different aspects of emotional intelligence
- Mastery of awareness-increasing instruments such as the *Emotional Competence Inventory* (ECI), the *Fundamental Inter-*

personal Relations Orientation–Behavior™ (FIRO-B®) instrument, and the *Myers-Briggs Type Indicator*® (MBTI®) personality inventory

- Understanding of change dynamics and processes

- Understanding of ARL principles and elements, which provide a framework for a wide variety of coaching interventions

- Depending on the context, other knowledge such as that related to leadership, teamwork, matrix organizations, organizational development, sustainability, large-scale change, cross-cultural topics, and so on

Required Mind-sets/Attitudes:

- Tolerance for silence, as reflection is an unusual practice and yet a powerful way to extract lessons

- Sense of humor, especially the ability to laugh at oneself

- Attention to body language

- Willingness to be transparent about what they are doing as well as how they are doing it

Teaching

Here we need to make a distinction between the content (what is being taught) and the process (how it is being taught).

Depending on the content, specific knowledge becomes important. Trainers in a corporate setting will have to teach content that is different from the content taught by college faculty. Presenters at a conference will have to cover a different content compared to the content taught by a task force team coach.

Given the fact that we are introducing ARL as a learning methodology applicable to a variety of adult learning scenarios, the content is as wide as the methodology's scope of application. However, considering the professional skills and knowledge that

Learning Coaches need to master, they already have significant potential content that can be transmitted via the teaching role. For example, a Learning Coach can intervene in a confusing meeting not only to implement a meeting management process (facilitator role) but also, adopting a teaching role, to teach the process so that participants will be able to apply it on their own. Or, seeing an opportunity to create a dialogue session (coaching role), the coach could not only set up the session but also explain (teaching role) what will be introduced, why it is a useful process, how it will be done, and how participants may use it. This way, the Learning Coach momentarily switches the coaching hat for the teaching hat and introduces a just-in-time process.

A subtle but important emphasis, central to the ARL approach, is that all the interventions, whether related to teaching, coaching, or facilitation, are seen as learning opportunities for creating awareness and transferring knowledge. By reviewing the inventory of knowledge and skills listed so far, it becomes clear that Learning Coaches in their teaching role have an extensive array of information to transfer. The way in which content is taught, however, is as important as mastering the subject.

Required Skills/Knowledge:

- Range of presentation skills, accommodating different learning styles

- Materials preparation

- Variety of approaches including active, reflective, concrete, and abstract activities to challenge and stimulate different learning styles

- Understanding of diversity (e.g., gender, ethnic, cultural, race, sexual orientation, and so on)

- Knowledge and understanding of ARL principles and elements

- Understanding of adult learning theories

Required Mind-sets/Attitudes:

- Comfort with an organic, just-in-time approach

- Newcomer learner attitude

- Open-mindedness, nonjudgmental attitude

Evaluation and Debrief

Discovery	Planning	Design and Redesign	Learning Interventions	Evaluation and Debrief

Evaluation is a process that runs through all phases. Ongoing feedback is needed in order to make corrections and adjustments, ensuring that expected outcomes are actually achieved as a result of the overall program.

Learning Coaches need an array of strategies and techniques for getting feedback. After feedback is received it must be analyzed, consolidated, shared, and applied. It is helpful to prepare thoughtful debriefs of evaluations, which can vary in length and format depending on the intensity, duration, and expectations of stakeholders. Every single intervention provides the coach with learning opportunities about the intervention's planning, design, and delivery. There is always something to learn. That is the good news for Learning Coaches—they will continue to be learning coaches.

Required Skills/Knowledge:

- Knowledge of and ability to manage strategies and methods for getting feedback—these include assessment tools, instruments, templates, questionnaires, surveys, interviews, and critical incident techniques

- Knowledge of different processes to assess and evaluate feedback

- Knowledge of different processes to conduct debrief sessions

Required Mind-sets/Attitudes:

- Openness to feedback
- Flexibility and openness to revisit and change assumptions, decisions, attitudes, contents, methodologies, or other aspects that have an impact on learning intervention results

SUMMING UP

This chapter has taken you through the intricacies and complexities of the Learning Coach role. You may have thought the role was alternately simple and easy and then complex and impossible to figure out, one moment obvious and familiar and the next moment deep and difficult. We have tried to describe and present the multiple facets of the ARL practitioner. An effective Learning Coach is like a human body that seems simple when it is healthy and working well but has an underlying complexity that requires exploration by scientists and researchers. Likewise, the interventions of the Learning Coach appear effortless when they work well yet are difficult to comprehend, describe, and explain. We still have a great deal to learn about the art and science of effective ARL coaching.

In applying this chapter to your practice, we invite you to lean toward the known and to take with you what is familiar from your organizational development experience, your teaching role, your coaching expertise, or your years of facilitating or consulting. Continue to build from there. Effective ARL practitioners have elements of all of these roles—facilitator, teacher, and coach. When Learning Coaches effectively and creatively combine these roles and apply the ARL principles and elements, they are able to inspire and support learning that lasts.

But remember, this combination is not a mechanistic process: it's not a series of techniques or a science that can guarantee predictable results in a given situation. As with all coaching, it is an art. As the practitioners who developed this approach have proved, it takes the courage to improvise and creatively bring the whole range of resources to bear to fit a particular situation and generate a unique intervention. Now that you've read, absorbed, and learned all of this, unleash the artist in yourself. Fly.

A Learning Story Revisited

After all the early morning hesitations and dialogue with himself, Jack decided to call Alicia and confirm that he would attend the negotiation course. A little sacrifice was worth the relationship with her, and he was somewhat intrigued about what he could learn on the topic.

He indeed learned a few techniques. He was lucky to have an entertaining instructor who kept the audience interested and laughing for almost two days. The instructor told stories, showed a movie, and showed numerous slides illustrating tricks and strategies for effective negotiation. Participants also had a chance to practice the techniques right away in several role-playing sessions.

At the end of the second workshop, though, Jack was eager to get back to his real life, to the accumulated work. He was not sure what he would use from everything he was learning. It was a lot to memorize, and, in addition, the examples were not very close to his context. True, the instructor asked for volunteers to present their challenges, but in that group of competitive colleagues, Jack didn't even think of serving as an example! He wondered if courses would be different one day, more applicable, more real . . .

We think that day has arrived. We hope that readers who have come to this page will have discovered something they can try out today. Maybe that reader is you.

As we unite our heart with our mind, and with our spirit, we honor ourselves, we honor each other, we honor all the teachers, and we honor all their teachings.

—Dina Glazer, Iyengar Yoga teacher

Notes

1. See Benjamin S. Bloom, *Taxonomy of Educational Objectives, Handbook 1: Cognitive Domain* (New York: Longman, 1956), 7.

2. See Peter Vail, *Learning as a Way of Being* (San Francisco: Jossey-Bass, 1996), 33.

3. See, for example, Peter Honey and Alan Mumford, *The Manual of Learning Styles* (Maidenhead, England: Peter Honey, 1992); Bernice McCarthy, *About Learning* (Barrington, IL: Excel, 1996); and David A. Kolb, *Experiential Learning: Experience as the Source of Learning and Development* (Englewood Cliffs, NJ: Prentice-Hall, 1984), 67.

4. See John Dewey, *Experience and Education* (New York: Collier Books, 1938).

5. Action Learning was originally developed by Reginald Revans in the United Kingdom in the 1940s. Individuals would meet in learning "sets" to work on current challenges, mainly by asking one another questions. The formula was $L = P + Q$, where L = learning, P = programmed contents, and Q = questioning.

6. This request is very similar to the way Action Learning programs are established, combining work on current challenges with learning. The difference in this case was mainly in the breadth and variety of roles the Learning Coaches played. For more on the roles of the Learning Coach, see chap. 13.

7. See Sharon D. Parks, *Leadership Can Be Taught* (Cambridge, MA: Harvard Business School Press, 2005), chap. 3.

8. For more information on the "4Mat" structure, see McCarthy, *About Learning*.

9. See Isabel Rimanoczy, "The Learning Cycle: Steps in the Process of Learning and Change," *Action Learning News* 23, no. 3 (September 2004): 2–10.

10. John Heider, *The Tao of Leadership: Lao Tzu's "Tao de Ching" Adapted for a New Age* (Atlanta: Horizons New Age, 1985), 17.

11. The *Myers-Briggs Type Indicator*® (MBTI®) instrument describes personality preferences.

12. "Interestingly, although the common focus and priority was the learning process, no one was connected to the pedagogic department of the university." Lennart Rohlin, personal communication, October 2006.

13. See Ivan Illich, *Deschooling Society* (New York: Harper & Row, 1970). Cited in Matthias Finger and José M. Asun, *Adult Education at the Crossroads: Learning Our Way Out* (London: Zed Books, 2001), introduction.

14. See Ivan Illich, *After Deschooling, What?* (London: Writers and Readers, 1973). Cited in Finger and Asun, *Adult Education at the Crossroads,* chap. 1.

15. See Lennart S. Rohlin, "Introducing MiL International Newsletter and Reporting from the EFMD Annual Conference, 1994," in "What Do We Mean by Action Reflection Learning?" *MiL Concepts* 1 (1996).

16. Early in 1981, thirteen members of this group took a research trip to the United States, visiting top management educational institutions in Boston (Boston Consulting Group, Harvard, Massachusetts Institute of Technology), New York (American Management Association, Aspen Institute, New York University, Tarrytown Executive Conference Center), Tucson (Motorola Institute, University of Arizona), northern California (Esalen Institute, Hewlett-Packard, Stanford University, University of California at Berkeley), and Los Angeles (University of California at Los Angeles, University of Southern California). See MiL Management Mission, *U.S. Trends in Management and Management Development* (Lund, Sweden: MiL Institute, 1982).

17. The MiL Institute is a Scandinavian not-for-profit foundation with around one hundred member corporations and seventy professional associates. It operates as a network for value-based and business-driven executive development.

18. See Reginald Revans, *The Origin and Growth of Action Learning* (London: Chartwell Bratt, 1982). Revans developed the formula $P + Q = L$, where P = programmed content, Q = questioning, and L = learning.

19. The term *Learning Coach* has since become more popular among Action Learning practitioners. The Learning Coach plays a wide variety of roles, yet the design of Action Learning programs has some specific characteristics. For an in-depth study of the roles of the Learning Coach in Action Learning programs, see Judy O'Neil, "The Role of the Learning Advisor in Action Learning," diss., Teachers College, Columbia University, 1999, 123; chap. 13 here describes in detail the roles of the Learning Coach within ARL. For a comparison of Action Learning and Action Reflection Learning, see Isabel Rimanoczy, "Action Learning and Action Reflection Learning: Are They Different?" *Industrial and Commercial Training* 39, nos. 5 and 6 (2007).

20. Lennart S. Rohlin et al., *Earning While Learning in Global Leadership: The Volvo MiL Partnership* (Vasbyholm, Sweden: MiL Publishers, 2002), 22.

21. The MiL Institute and its sister organization in the United States, LIM (Leadership in International Management), jointly came up with this designation.

22. See Rohlin et al., *Earning While Learning in Global Leadership*.

23. Isabel Rimanoczy conducted a qualitative, exploratory study with twenty-three practitioners in nine different locations. See Paul Roberts, Isabel Rimanoczy, and Boris Drizin, "Principles and Elements of ARL," *MiL Concepts* 1 (2007).

24. We want to mention here the pioneering work of scholars Victoria Marsick, Lyle Yorks, Sharon Lamm, Bob Kolodny, Glenn Nilson, and Judy O'Neil, who researched different aspects of ARL as visiting scholars at the MiL Institute and also as members of the ARL Inquiry research group.

25. See Isabel Rimanoczy, "Principios y Elementos de Action Reflection Learning," diss., Universidad de Palermo, Buenos Aires, 2005. A description of the study and its findings is also in Roberts, Rimanoczy, and Drizin, "Principles and Elements of ARL."

26. While instructional design professionals may be more familiar with the ADDIE Model (Analyze needs, Design learning objectives, Develop materials and methods, Implement the program, and Evaluate how objectives have been met), we prefer a less linear model that allows us to follow the organic flow of the learning process, with frequent evaluations that result in ongoing redesign.

27. A Learning Coach who uses the Stop, Reflect, Write, Report technique invites the learner to engage in a moment of silent reflection, write down the answer to a specific question, and then share it.

28. The World Café is a conversation technique developed by Juanita Brown and David Isaacs. See www.theworldcafe.com.

29. See Donna M. Smith and David A. Kolb, *The User's Guide for the Learning-Style Inventory: A Manual for Teachers and Trainers* (Boston: McBer, 1986); and McCarthy, *About Learning*. The *Emotional Competence Inventory* was developed by the Hay Group. The FIRO-B® instrument (Mountain View, CA: CPP, Inc.) assesses interpersonal needs and how they affect interactions. On the MBTI® instrument, see Isabel B. Myers, *Myers-Briggs Type Indicator®* (Mountain View, CA: CPP, Inc., 1962).

30. For a more detailed description of the Learning Coach roles, see chap. 13.

31. See Michael Polanyi, *Personal Knowledge: Towards a Post-Critical Philosophy* (London: Routledge, 1958), 69–123.

32. See Etienne Wenger, *Communities of Practice: Learning, Meaning and Identity* (Cambridge: Cambridge University Press, 1998), chap. 6.

33. See Ikujiro Nonaka, "The Knowledge-Creating Company," *Harvard Business Review* (November–December 1991): 96–104.

34. Thomas A. Stewart, *Intellectual Capital: The New Wealth of Organizations* (New York: Doubleday, 1997), chap. 5.

35. See Stephen Brookfield, *Becoming a Critically Reflective Teacher* (San Francisco: Jossey-Bass, 1995); and Jack Mezirow, *Learning as Transformation: Critical Perspectives on a Theory in Progress* (San Francisco: Jossey-Bass, 2000), 9–21, 45–48.

36. See Stephen Brookfield, "Developing Critically Reflective Practitioners: A Rationale for Training Educators of Adults," in *Training Educators of Adults: The Theory and Practice of Graduate Adult Education* (New York: Routledge, 1988), 325.

37. Jack Mezirow, *Fostering Critical Reflection in Adulthood* (San Francisco: Jossey-Bass, 1990), 5.

38. Cognitive psychology is the school of psychology that examines internal mental processes such as problem solving, memory, and language. It is built on the Gestalt psychology of Max Wertheimer, Wolfgang Köhler, and Kurt Koffka and the work of Jean Piaget.

39. See John Dewey, *Democracy and Education: An Introduction to the Philosophy of Education* (New York: Free Press, 1916), 186–201; and *Experience and Education.*

40. Kolb, *Experiential Learning,* 21.

41. See Isabel Rimanoczy, "The Learning Cycle: Steps in the Process of Learning and Change," *Action Learning News* 23, no. 3 (September 2004): 2–10.

42. See Kurt Lewin, *Field Theory in Social Science* (New York: Harper, 1951).

43. See Chris Argyris, *Reasoning, Learning and Action: Individual and Organizational* (San Francisco: Jossey-Bass, 1982), 67–91.

44. Donald Schön, *The Reflective Practitioner: How Professionals Think in Action* (New York: Basic Books, 1983), chaps. 1 and 2.

45. See, e.g., John B. Watson, *Behaviorism* (1925; reprint New York: W. W. Norton and Company, 1970); Edward L. Thorndike, *The Fundamentals of Learning* (New York: Bureau of Publications, Teachers College, Columbia University, 1932); B. F. Skinner, *Beyond Freedom and Dignity* (New York: Alfred A. Knopf, 1971), and *About Behaviorism* (New York: Alfred A. Knopf, 1974). For information on Ivan Pavlov, see, e.g., David

Hothersall, *History of Psychology* (New York: McGraw-Hill, 1995), 239–253.

46. Edward Thorndike, *The Fundamentals of Learning* (New York: Teachers College Press, 1932).

47. See David P. Ausubel, Joseph D. Novak, and H. Hanesian, *Educational Psychology: A Cognitive View,* 2nd ed. (New York: Holt, Rinehart & Winston, 1978).

48. See John Dewey, *Human Nature and Conduct: An Introduction to Social Psychology* (New York: Random House, 1922), 69–75.

49. See William James, *The Principles of Psychology* (1890; reprint Cambridge, MA: Harvard University Press, 1981).

50. See Mezirow, *Learning as Transformation,* chap. 1.

51. See Egon G. Guba and Yvonna S. Lincoln, "Competing Paradigms in Qualitative Research," in *The Landscape of Qualitative Research: Theories and Issues,* ed. Norman K. Denzin and Yvonna S. Lincoln, 195–220 (Thousand Oaks, CA: Sage, 1998).

52. Thomas S. Kuhn, *The Structure of Scientific Revolutions,* 2nd ed. (Chicago: University of Chicago Press, 1970), 175.

53. See W. M. Trochim, *The Research Methods Knowledge Base,* 2nd ed. http://trochim.human.cornell.edu/kb/index.htm (accessed January 16, 2005).

54. See Guba and Lincoln, "Competing Paradigms in Qualitative Research," 195–220.

55. See Wilfred Carr and Stephen Kemmis, *Becoming Critical: Education, Knowledge and Action Research* (London: Falmer, 1986).

56. See Jack Mezirow, *Transformative Dimensions of Adult Learning* (San Francisco: Jossey-Bass, 1991), chap. 5.

57. Henry D. Thoreau, *Walden, or, Life in the Woods* (Stigiwil, KS: Digireads.com Publishing, 2005), 153.

58. See, e.g., Argyris, *Reasoning, Learning and Action;* Schön, *The Reflective Practitioner;* Peter Senge, *The Fifth Discipline* (New York: Doubleday, 1990); Gareth Morgan, *Images of Organization* (London: Sage, 1997); Patricia Cranton, *Understanding and Promoting Transformative Learning* (San Francisco: Jossey-Bass, 1994); and Mezirow, *Transformative Dimensions of Adult Learning.*

59. On education and social action, see Paulo Freire, *Pedagogy of the Oppressed* (New York: Seabury, 1970); and Myles Horton and Paulo Freire, *We Make the Road by Walking: Conversations on Education and Social Change* (Philadelphia: Temple University Press, 1990). On education and feminism, see Mary F. Belenky et al., eds., *Women's Ways of Knowing* (New York: Basic Books, 1986).

60. See Kenneth Gergen, *An Invitation to Social Construction* (London: Sage, 1999), 33–61; and Freire, *Pedagogy of the Oppressed.*

61. See Lev S. Vygotsky, *Thought and Language* (Cambridge, MA: MIT Press, 1962), and *Mind in Society* (Cambridge, MA: Harvard University Press, 1978).

62. See Jean Lave and Etienne Wenger, *Situated Learning: Legitimate Peripheral Participation* (Cambridge: Cambridge University Press, 1990).

63. See Wenger, *Communities of Practice,* 13.

64. See Jean Lave, *Cognition in Practice: Mind, Mathematics, and Culture in Everyday Life* (Cambridge: Cambridge University Press, 1988), 55–63.

65. Albert Bandura, *Social Learning Theory* (Englewood Cliffs, NJ: Prentice-Hall, 1977), 22.

66. See, e.g., Albert Bandura, *Self-efficacy: The Exercise of Control* (New York: W. H. Freeman, 1997), 1–45.

67. See Revans, *Origin and Growth of Action Learning.*

68. See, e.g., Victoria J. Marsick and Judy O'Neil, "The Many Faces of Action Learning," *Management Learning* 30, no. 2 (1999): 159–76; Joseph A. Raelin, *Work-Based Learning: The New Frontier of Management Development* (Upper Saddle River, NJ: Prentice-Hall, 2000); Nancy M. Dixon, "Action Learning: More Than Just a Task Force," *Performance Improvement Quarterly* 11, no. 1 (1998): 45–58; Michael J. Marquardt, *Action Learning in Action: Transforming Problems and People for World-Class Organizational Learning* (Mountain View, CA: Davies-Black Publishing, 1999), 26; David L. Dotlich and James L. Noel, *Action Learning: How the World's Top Companies Are Re-Creating Their Leaders and Themselves* (San Francisco: Jossey-Bass, 1998); Ian McGill and Liz Beaty, *Action Learning: A Practitioner's Guide* (London: Kogan Page, 1997); and M. Pedler, ed., *Action Learning in Practice,* 3rd ed. (Aldershot, Hants, England: Gower, 1997).

69. For cognitive psychology, see Jean Piaget, "Intellectual Evolution from Adolescence to Adulthood," *Human Development* 16 (1972): 346–70. For humanistic-oriented theory, see C. Rogers, *On Becoming a Person: A Therapist's View of Psychotherapy* (Boston: Houghton Mifflin, 1961); and Malcolm S. Knowles, *The Modern Practice of Adult Education: Andragogy Versus Pedagogy* (New York: Association Press, 1970). For critical theory, see Freire, *Pedagogy of the Oppressed;* Horton and Freire, *We Make the Road by Walking;* and Philip C. Candy and Stephen D. Brookfield, *Self-direction for Lifelong Learning: A Comprehensive Guide to Theory and Practice* (San Francisco: Jossey-Bass, 1991). For learning theory, see Kolb, *Experiential Learning;* Mezirow, *Learning as Transformation;* Schön, *The Reflective Practitioner;* and Cranton, *Understanding and Promoting Transformative Learning.*

70. See Edgar H. Schein, *Process Consultation: Its Role in Organizational Development* (Reading, MA: Addison-Wesley, 1988).

71. See Revans, *Origin and Growth of Action Learning.*

72. See Judy O'Neil, "Set Advising: More Than Just Process Consultancy?" in *Action Learning in Practice,* ed. Mike Pedler, 243–256.

73. On the use of probing questions, see Marquardt, *Action Learning in Action,* and *Leading with Questions: How Leaders Find the Right Solutions by Knowing What to Ask* (San Francisco: Jossey-Bass, 2005).

74. See Vail, *Learning as a Way of Being,* 25–50.

75. See Freire, *Pedagogy of the Oppressed,* 71–86.

76. See Cranton, *Understanding and Promoting Transformative Learning,* chap. 1.

77. See John Dewey, *How We Think: A Restatement of the Relation of Reflective Thinking to the Educative Process* (Boston: D. C. Heath, 1933); Eduard C. Lindeman, *The Meaning of Adult Education* (New York: New Republic, 1926); and Kolb, *Experiential Learning.*

78. On situated learning, see Vygotsky, *Thought and Language.* On Action Learning, see Revans, *Origin and Growth of Action Learning.*

79. See Knowles, *Modern Practice of Adult Education,* 40–60.

80. See Kath Murdoch, *Classroom Connections: Strategies for Integrated Learning* (Armadale, Australia: Eleanor Curtin, 1998); and Kath Murdoch and Jeni Wilson, *Learning Links: Strategic Teaching for the Learner-Centered Classroom* (Carlton South, Australia: Curriculum Corporation, 2004).

81. See Kurt Lewin, *Resolving Social Conflicts: Selected Papers on Group Dynamics.* Ed. Gertrude W. Lewin (New York: Harper & Row, 1948).

82. Lave, *Cognition in Practice.*

83. See Raelin, *Work-Based Learning.*

84. See Rogers, *On Becoming a Person.*

85. See Daniel Goleman, *Emotional Intelligence* (London: Bloomsbury, 1996).

86. See Ken Wilber, *A Theory of Everything* (Dublin: Gateway, 2001).

87. See Elizabeth Tisdell, *Exploring Spirituality and Culture in Adult and Higher Education* (San Francisco: Jossey-Bass, 2003).

88. See David L. Cooperrider and Diana Whitney, "Appreciative Inquiry: A Positive Revolution in Change," in *The Change Handbook,* ed. Peggy Holman and Tom Devane, 245–263 (San Francisco: Berrett-Koehler, 1999).

89. Social Constructionism is a sociological theory of knowledge that looks into the way individuals and groups participate in the creation of their perceived reality. The concept was introduced in the United States in

1967 by Peter Berger and Thomas Luckmann in *The Social Construction of Reality: A Treatise in the Sociology of Knowledge* (Garden City, NY: Doubleday, 1967).

90. Cooperrider and Whitney, "Appreciative Inquiry," 246.

91. See James, *Principles of Psychology.*

92. See Sigmund Freud, *The Basic Writings of Sigmund Freud* (New York: Random House, 1995).

93. See Carl Jung, *Psychological Types* (1921, reprint Princeton, NJ: Princeton University Press, 1971); and Isabel B. Myers, *Myers-Briggs Type Indicator®* (Mountain View, CA: CPP, Inc., 1962).

94. See Senge, *Fifth Discipline,* 139–173.

95. See Goleman, *Emotional Intelligence.*

96. See Mezirow, *Fostering Critical Reflection in Adulthood,* and *Transformative Dimensions of Adult Learning.*

97. See Freire, *Pedagogy of the Oppressed;* Argyris, *Reasoning, Learning and Action;* Schön, *Reflective Practitioner;* Brookfield, "Developing Critically Reflective Practitioners"; Cranton, *Understanding and Promoting Transformative Learning;* and Robert Kegan and Lisa Lahey, *How the Way We Talk Can Change the Way We Work* (San Francisco: Jossey-Bass, 2001).

98. See Ludwig von Bertalanffy, *General System Theory: Foundations, Development, Application* (New York: Braziller, 1968).

99. See Fritjof Capra, *The Web of Life: A New Scientific Understanding of Living Systems* (New York: Anchor Books, 1996), and *The Hidden Connections: Integrating the Biological, Cognitive, and Social Dimensions of Life into a Science of Sustainability* (New York: Anchor Books/Random House, 2001).

100. Lewin, *Field Theory in Social Science,* 240.

101. For the application of systemic thinking in sociology, see Michael C. Jackson, *Systems Methodology for the Management Sciences* (New York: Plenum Press, 1991). In political science and social action, see Alice M. Rivlin, *Systematic Thinking for Social Action* (Washington, DC: Brookings Institution Press, 1971). In business, management, and organizational theory, see Senge, *Fifth Discipline;* and John D. Sterman, *Business Dynamics: Systems Thinking and Modeling for a Complex World* (Columbus, OH: McGraw-Hill, 2000). In psychotherapy, see Stephen J. Schultz, *Family Systems Thinking* (Northvale, NJ: Jason Aronson, 1993). In economics, see Bernard Hodgson, *Economics as Moral Science* (New York: Springer, 2001). In ecology, see Capra, *Web of Life* and *Hidden Connections.*

102. See John Elkington, *Cannibals with Forks: The Triple Bottom Line in the 21st Century Business* (Oxford: Capstone, 1998); Paul Hawken, *The Ecology of Commerce: How Business Can Save the Planet* (Phoenix, AZ: Harper-Collins, 1993); and Paul Hawken, Amory B. Lovins, and L. Hunter Lovins, *Natural Capitalism: Creating the Next Industrial Revolution* (London: Earthscan Publications, 1999).

103. The term *Learning Coach* was first used by MiL and LIM in the mid-1990s to identify the specialized role of facilitator of their ARL programs. At their inception, LIM's and MiL's programs adhered more to traditional Action Learning interventions, and facilitators were called PTAs (project team advisors). However, ARL practitioners moved spontaneously beyond the hitherto accepted Action Learning conventions, and the PTA title was no longer seen as adequate. Further, the need to transfer professional expertise to newcomers forced LIM and MiL to explore and identify the competencies, skills, and knowledge bases of ARL practitioners. Since then, the term *Learning Coach* has been adopted by many Action Learning practitioners. For a full comparison of Action Learning and Action Reflection Learning, see Isabel Rimanoczy, "Action Learning and Action Reflection Learning: Are They Different?"

104. See John Heron, *Co-operative Inquiry: Research into the Human Condition* (London: Sage, 1996), 73–100.

105. Note that what we depict here as underlying the Learning Coach's interventions also applies to what underlies the learner's actions, as we all, Learning Coach or not, share these dynamics of knowledge, experience, values, and personal characteristics.

106. See Robert Kegan, *In Over Our Heads: The Mental Demands of Modern Life* (Cambridge, MA: Harvard University Press, 1994).

References

Argyris, Chris. *Reasoning, Learning and Action: Individual and Organizational.* San Francisco: Jossey-Bass, 1982.

Ausubel, David P., Joseph D. Novak, and H. Hanesian. *Educational Psychology: A Cognitive View.* 2nd ed. New York: Holt, Rinehart & Winston, 1978.

Bandura, Albert. *Self-efficacy: The Exercise of Control.* New York: W. H. Freeman, 1997.

———. *Social Learning Theory.* Englewood Cliffs, NJ: Prentice-Hall, 1977.

Belenky, Mary, B. Clinchy, Nancy Goldberger, and Jill Tarule, eds. *Women's Ways of Knowing.* New York: Basic Books, 1986.

Berger, Peter L., and Thomas Luckmann. *The Social Construction of Reality: A Treatise in the Sociology of Knowledge.* Garden City, NY: Doubleday, 1967.

Bertalanffy, Ludwig von. *General System Theory: Foundations, Development, Application.* New York: Braziller, 1968.

Bloom, Benjamin S. *Taxonomy of Educational Objectives, Handbook 1: Cognitive Domain.* New York: Longman, 1956.

Brookfield, Stephen. *Becoming a Critically Reflective Teacher.* San Francisco: Jossey-Bass, 1995.

———. "Developing Critically Reflective Practitioners: A Rationale for Training Educators of Adults." In *Training Educators of Adults: The Theory and Practice of Graduate Adult Education.* New York: Routledge, 1988.

Candy, Philip C., and Stephen D. Brookfield. *Self-direction for Lifelong Learning: A Comprehensive Guide to Theory and Practice.* San Francisco: Jossey-Bass, 1991.

Capra, Fritjof. *The Hidden Connections: Integrating the Biological, Cognitive, and Social Dimensions of Life into a Science of Sustainability.* New York: Anchor Books/Random House, 2001.

———. *The Web of Life: A New Scientific Understanding of Living Systems.* New York: Anchor Books, 1996.

Carr, Wilfred, and Stephen Kemmis. *Becoming Critical: Education, Knowledge and Action Research.* London: Falmer, 1986.

Cooperrider, David L., and Diana Whitney. "Appreciative Inquiry: A Positive Revolution in Change." In *The Change Handbook,* ed. Peggy Holman and Tom Devane, 245–263. San Francisco: Berrett-Koehler, 1999.

Cranton, Patricia. *Understanding and Promoting Transformative Learning.* San Francisco: Jossey-Bass, 1994.

Dewey, John. *Democracy and Education: An Introduction to the Philosophy of Education.* New York: Free Press, 1916.

————. *Experience and Education.* New York: Collier Books, 1938.

————. *How We Think: A Restatement of the Relation of Reflective Thinking to the Educative Process.* Boston: D. C. Heath, 1933.

————. *Human Nature and Conduct: An Introduction to Social Psychology.* New York: Random House, 1922.

Dixon, Nancy M. "Action Learning: More Than Just a Task Force." *Performance Improvement Quarterly* 11, no. 1 (1998): 45–58.

Dotlich, David L., and James L. Noel. *Action Learning: How the World's Top Companies Are Re-Creating Their Leaders and Themselves.* San Francisco: Jossey-Bass, 1998.

Elkington, John. *Cannibals with Forks: The Triple Bottom Line in the 21st Century Business.* Oxford: Capstone, 1998.

Finger, Matthias, and José M. Asun. *Adult Education at the Crossroads: Learning Our Way Out.* London: Zed Books, 2001.

Freire, Paulo. *Pedagogy of the Oppressed.* New York: Seabury, 1970.

Freud, Sigmund. *The Basic Writings of Sigmund Freud.* New York: Random House, 1995.

Gergen, Kenneth. *An Invitation to Social Construction.* London: Sage, 1999.

Gilligan, Carol. *In a Different Voice.* Cambridge, MA: Harvard University Press, 1982.

Goleman, Daniel. *Emotional Intelligence.* London: Bloomsbury Publishing, 1996.

Guba, Egon G., and Yvonna S. Lincoln. "Competing Paradigms in Qualitative Research." In *The Landscape of Qualitative Research: Theories and Issues,* ed. N. K. Denzin and Y. S. Lincoln, 195–220. Thousand Oaks, CA: Sage, 1998.

Hawken, Paul. *The Ecology of Commerce: How Business Can Save the Planet.* Phoenix, AZ: Harper-Collins, 1993.

Hawken, Paul, Amory B. Lovins, and L. Hunter Lovins. *Natural Capitalism.* London: Earthscan Publications, 1999.

Heider, John. *The Tao of Leadership: Leadership Strategies for a New Age.* Atlanta: Bantam Books, 1986.

Heron, John. *Co-operative Inquiry: Research into the Human Condition.* London: Sage, 1996.

Hodgson, Bernard. *Economics as Moral Science.* New York: Springer, 2001.

Honey, Peter, and Alan Mumford. *The Manual of Learning Styles.* Maidenhead, England: Peter Honey, 1992.

Horton, Myles, and Paulo Freire. *We Make the Road by Walking: Conversations on Education and Social Change.* Philadelphia: Temple University Press, 1990.

Hothersall, David. *History of Psychology.* New York: McGraw-Hill, 1995.

Illich, Ivan. *After Deschooling, What?* London: Writers & Readers, 1973.

————. *Deschooling Society.* New York: Harper & Row, 1970.

Jackson, Michael C. *Systems Methodology for the Management Sciences.* New York: Plenum Press, 1991.

James, William. *The Principles of Psychology*. 1890. Cambridge, MA: Harvard University Press, 1981.

Jung, Carl. *Psychological Types*. 1921. Princeton, NJ: Princeton University Press, 1971.

Kegan, Robert. *In Over Our Heads: The Mental Demands of Modern Life*. Cambridge, MA: Harvard University Press, 1994.

Kegan, Robert, and Lisa Lahey. *How the Way We Talk Can Change the Way We Work*. San Francisco: Jossey-Bass, 2001.

Knowles, Malcolm S. *The Modern Practice of Adult Education: Andragogy Versus Pedagogy*. New York: Association Press, 1970.

Kolb, David A. *Experiential Learning: Experience as the Source of Learning and Development*. Englewood Cliffs, NJ: Prentice-Hall, 1984.

———. *Learning-Style Inventory*. Boston: McBer, 1976.

Kuhn, Thomas S. *The Structure of Scientific Revolutions*. 2nd ed. Chicago: University of Chicago Press, 1970.

Lave, Jean. *Cognition in Practice: Mind, Mathematics, and Culture in Everyday Life*. Cambridge: Cambridge University Press, 1988.

Lave, Jean, and Etienne Wenger. *Situated Learning: Legitimate Peripheral Participation*. Cambridge: Cambridge University Press, 1990.

Lewin, Kurt. *Field Theory in Social Science: Selected Theoretical Papers*. Ed. Dorwin Cartwright. New York: Harper & Row, 1951.

———. *Resolving Social Conflicts: Selected Papers on Group Dynamics*. Ed. Gertrude W. Lewin. New York: Harper & Row, 1948.

Lindeman, Eduard C. *The Meaning of Adult Education*. New York: New Republic, 1926.

Marquardt, Michael J. *Action Learning in Action: Transforming Problems and People for World-Class Organizational Learning*. Mountain View, CA: Davies-Black Publishing, 1999.

———. *Leading with Questions: How Leaders Find the Right Solutions by Knowing What to Ask*. San Francisco: Jossey-Bass, 2005.

Marsick, Victoria J., and Judy O'Neil. "The Many Faces of Action Learning." *Management Learning* 30, no. 2 (1999): 159–76.

McCarthy, Bernice. *About Learning*. Barrington, IL: Excel, 1996.

McGill, Ian, and Liz Beaty. *Action Learning: A Practitioner's Guide*. London: Kogan Page, 1997.

Mezirow, Jack. *Fostering Critical Reflection in Adulthood*. San Francisco: Jossey-Bass, 1990.

———. *Learning as Transformation*. San Francisco: Jossey-Bass, 2000.

———. *Transformative Dimensions of Adult Learning*. San Francisco: Jossey-Bass, 1991.

MiL Management Mission. *U.S. Trends in Management and Management Development*. Lund, Sweden: MiL Institute, 1982.

Morgan, Gareth. *Images of Organization*. London: Sage, 1997.

Murdoch, Kath. *Classroom Connections: Strategies for Integrated Learning*. Armadale, Australia: Eleanor Curtin, 1998.

Murdoch, Kath, and Jeni Wilson. *Learning Links: Strategic Teaching for the Learner-Centered Classroom.* Carlton South, Australia: Curriculum Corporation, 2004.

Myers, Isabel B. *Myers-Briggs Type Indicator®.* Mountain View, CA: CPP, Inc., 1962.

Nonaka, Ikujiro. "The Knowledge-Creating Company." *Harvard Business Review* (November–December 1991): 96–104.

O'Neil, Judy. "The Role of the Learning Advisor in Action Learning." Doctoral diss., Teachers College, Columbia University, 1999.

———. "Set Advising: More Than Just Process Consultancy?" In *Action Learning in Practice,* ed. Mike Pedler, 243–56. 3rd ed. Aldershot, Hants, England: Gower, 1997.

Parks, Sharon D. *Leadership Can Be Taught.* Cambridge, MA: Harvard Business School Press, 2005.

Pedler, Mike, ed. *Action Learning in Practice.* 3rd ed. Aldershot, Hants, England: Gower, 1997.

Piaget, Jean. "Intellectual Evolution from Adolescence to Adulthood." *Human Development* 16 (1972): 346–70.

———. *The Origins of Intelligence.* New York: International University Press, 1952.

Polanyi, Michael. *Personal Knowledge: Towards a Post-Critical Philosophy.* London: Routledge, 1958.

———. *The Tacit Dimension.* Garden City, NY: Doubleday, 1966.

Raelin, Joseph A. *Work-Based Learning: The New Frontier of Management Development.* Upper Saddle River, NJ: Prentice-Hall, 2000.

———. "Work-Based Learning in Practice." *Journal of Workplace Learning* 10, no. 6/7 (1998): 280–83.

Revans, Reginald. *The Origin and Growth of Action Learning.* London: Chartwell Bratt, 1982.

Rimanoczy, Isabel. "Action Learning and Action Reflection Learning: Are They Different?" *Industrial and Commercial Training* 39, nos. 5 and 6 (2007).

———. "The Learning Cycle: Steps in the Process of Learning and Change." *Action Learning News* 23, no. 3 (September 2004): 2–10.

———. "Principios y Elementos de Action Reflection Learning." Diss., Universidad de Palermo, Buenos Aires, 2005.

Rimanoczy, Isabel, Ernie Turner, and Tony Pearson. *Learning Coach Handbook Internal Publication.* www.limglobal.net (accessed 2000).

Rivlin, Alice M. *Systematic Thinking for Social Action.* Washington, DC: Brookings Institution Press, 1971.

Roberts, Paul, Isabel Rimanoczy, and Boris Drizin. "Principles and Elements of ARL." *MiL Concepts* 1 (2007).

Rogers, Carl. *On Becoming a Person: A Therapist's View of Psychotherapy.* Boston: Houghton Mifflin, 1961.

Rogers, Carl, and H. J. Freiberg. *Freedom to Learn.* 3rd ed. New York: Merrill, 1993.

Rohlin, Lennart. "Introducing MiL International Newsletter and Reporting from the EFMD Annual Conference 1994." In "What Do We Mean by Action Reflection Learning?" *MiL Concepts* 1 (1996).

Rohlin, Lennart, Sven A. Nilsson, and Per-Hugo Skärvad. *Strategic Leadership in the Learning Society.* Lund, Sweden: MiL Publishers, 1998.

Rohlin, Lennart, Mikael Wickelgren, Eva Arnell, Ernie Turner, Thomas Sewerin, Sharon Lamm, Inger Draeby, Bill Braddick, Lars Cederholm, Øystein Rennemo, Åse Hagerstrom, Victoria J. Marsick, Anders Boglind, and Agneta Karlsson. *Earning While Learning in Global Leadership: The Volvo MiL Partnership.* Vasbyholm, Sweden: MiL Publishers, 2002.

Schein, Edgar H. *Process Consultation: Its Role in Organizational Development.* Reading, MA: Addison-Wesley, 1988.

Schön, Donald. *The Reflective Practitioner.* New York: Basic Books, 1983.

Schultz, Stephen J. *Family Systems Thinking.* Northvale, NJ: Jason Aronson, 1993.

Senge, Peter. *The Fifth Discipline.* New York: Doubleday, 1990.

Skinner, B. F. *About Behaviorism.* New York: Alfred A. Knopf, 1974.

———. *Beyond Freedom and Dignity.* New York: Alfred A. Knopf, 1971.

Smith, Donna, and David A. Kolb. *The User's Guide for the Learning-Style Inventory: A Manual for Teachers and Trainers.* Boston: McBer, 1986.

Sterman, John D. *Business Dynamics: Systems Thinking and Modeling for a Complex World.* Columbus, OH: McGraw-Hill, 2000.

Stewart, T. A. *Intellectual Capital: The New Wealth of Organizations.* New York: Doubleday, 1997.

Thoreau, Henry D. *Walden, or Life in the Woods.* Stigiwil, KS: Digireads.com Publishing, 2005.

Thorndike, Edward L. *The Fundamentals of Learning.* New York, Bureau of Publications, Teachers College, Columbia University, 1932.

Tisdell, Elizabeth. *Exploring Spirituality and Culture in Adult and Higher Education.* San Francisco: Jossey-Bass, 2003.

Trochim, William M. *The Research Methods Knowledge Base.* 2nd ed. http://trochim. human.cornell.edu/kb/index.htm (accessed January 16, 2005).

Vail, Peter. *Learning as a Way of Being.* San Francisco: Jossey-Bass, 1996.

Vygotsky, Lev S. *Mind in Society.* Cambridge, MA: Harvard University Press, 1978.

———. *Thought and Language.* Cambridge, MA: MIT Press, 1962.

Watson, John B. *Behaviorism.* 1925. Reprint. New York: W. W. Norton & Company, 1970.

Wenger, Etienne. *Communities of Practice: Learning, Meaning and Identity.* Cambridge: Cambridge University Press, 1998.

Wilber, Ken. *A Theory of Everything.* Dublin: Gateway, 2001.

Index

Action Learning, 190, 193

Action Reflection Learning: in academic settings, 140; applications of, 14, 140–142; characteristics of, 15; classroom-style learning vs., 15; defining of, 142; in education, 47–65; evolution of, 13–14, 135–143; history of, 13; MiL model and, 137–140; origins of, 135–143; results of, 28; schematic diagram of, 7

action research, 178

active inquirer, 195

Affective Domain, 8, 10

andragogy, 195–196

applied learning, 25

appreciative approach: assumptions of, 180, 197, 201; in cascading change case study, 110, 129; in coaching case study, 80; definition of, 155; description of, 23, 30, 37, 40; in education case study, 52; implementation by Learning Coach, 155–156; integration and, 197; in leadership transition case study, 37; in merger case study, 23; repetition and reinforcement and, 180; in sales force case study, 72; self-awareness and, 201; in team turnaround case study, 96, 100–101, 103

Appreciative Inquiry, 198–199

Argyris, Chris, 178

assumption analysis, 176

automatic learning, 7, 11–13

awareness, 129

balancing task and learning: assumptions of, 194; in cascading change case study, 111–112, 117; in coaching case study, 78–79; definition of, 156; description of, 21, 30, 45; in education case study, 60; implementation by Learning Coach, 156–157; in leadership

transition case study, 39; in merger case study, 21; relevance and, 194; in sales force case study, 72; in team turnaround case study, 98, 103

Bandura, Albert, 180, 189–190

Bateson, Gregory, 203

behavioral psychology, 179

behaviorism, 180–181

Bloom, Benjamin, 8

Briggs, Katharine, 200

Brookfield, Stephen, 176

cascading change case study, 107–132

case studies: cascading change, 107–132; coaching, 77–88; education, 47–66; HR, 67–70; leadership transition, 33–41; merger, 19–29; sales force, 70–73; team turnaround, 89–105

change cycle, 178

classroom-style learning: Action Reflection Learning vs., 15; description of, 10

coaching case study, 77–78

Cognitive Domain, 8, 10

cognitive psychology, 177

contextual awareness, 177

Cooperrider, David, 198–199

Critical Incident question, 154

critical reflection, 175–177

cross-cultural relationships, 40

cybernetics, 203

design and redesign stage of learning: description of, 148, 159; Learning Coach in, 220–221

Dewey, John, 11, 180, 195

directive approaches, 192

discipline, 26

discovery stage of learning: description of, 148, 159; Learning Coach in, 217–219

double-loop learning, 178

Drizin, Boris, 145, 171–172, 206

LIM

LEADERSHIP IN INTERNATIONAL MANAGEMENT

Founded in 1986 in the U.S., LIM, Leadership in International Management LLC, is a consulting firm that specializes in leadership and team development. With a network of certified Learning Coaches in North and South America, Europe, and Asia, LIM uses the ARL principles and elements in the design and delivery of all its interventions.

Visit www.LIMglobal.net and subscribe to the monthly electronic newsletter *LIM News,* edited by author Isabel Rimanoczy, featuring short, cutting-edge articles on a variety of leadership challenges.

If you want to develop your ARL coaching skills, enroll in the ARL Academy, where you will learn how to design and deliver ARL-based learning interventions in the ARL Certificate Program.

For more information visit www.actionreflectionlearning.com/academy, or e-mail info@actionreflectionlearning.com